BASEBALL IN SAN DIEGO

FROM THE PLAZA TO THE PADRES

This book is dedicated to a bunch of old-timers who once were youngsters playing baseball on San Diego's dirt diamonds. Their help with this book has been invaluable. Among those who played ball in the 1920s were Pete Grijalva, Athos Sada, and Al Storton. Pete died in 2004 at 97 years of age. Players from the 1930s include Johnny "Swede" Jensen, Frank Kerr, Pete Coscarart, Ted Williams, Ed Sanclemente, Walter McCoy, Ernie Beck, Johnny Ritchey, Danny Millsap, and Bill and Mel Skelley. Frank Kerr died in 2000, Pete Coscarart and Ted Williams in 2002, Johnny Ritchey in 2003, and Mel Skelley in 2004. Danny Millsap died in 2005. Al Storton is shown above in 1922 with Miss Bone and her fifth grade team at Brooklyn Elementary School. On the right, Mel Skelley is swinging his bat in 1928 at Balboa Park. Our best memories of baseball are from when we were kids. We played every chance we had . . .

BASEBALL IN SAN DIEGO

FROM THE PLAZA TO THE PADRES

Bill Swank
in conjunction with the San Diego Historical Society

ARCADIA

Published by Arcadia Publishing
Charleston SC, Chicago IL, Portsmouth NH, San Francisco CA

Printed in Great Britain

Library of Congress Catalog Card Number: 2005921467

For all general information contact Arcadia Publishing at:
Telephone 843-853-2070
Fax 843-853-0044
E-mail sales@arcadiapublishing.com
For customer service and orders:
Toll-Free 1-888-313-2665

Visit us on the internet at http://www.arcadiapublishing.com

ACKNOWLEDGMENTS

Special recognition is given the following work that served as road signs along the way: *Always on Sunday* by John Spalding, *The California Winter League* by William McNeil and *Caver Conquest* by Don King. Every San Diego sports fan should have Don's history of San Diego High School athletics on their bookshelf. Over twenty years ago, Frank Norris wrote a fine article about early San Diego baseball in *The Journal of San Diego History*. Prehistorian Angus Macfarlane has dug deep to find old base ball DNA in the Golden State. High fives to all of you.

Thanks goes to Roger Showley who waved good bye when I departed Horton Plaza in 1871. Dennis Sharp and Carol Myers were always available to provide assistance at the San Diego Historical Society. Though he didn't realize it, Dennis provided the most encouragement for this project. This has been a shared venture with the San Diego Historical Society. Tom Larwin graciously gave information about the original San Diego Bears and Pickwicks from the early 20th century. Finally, every author would want teammates like Arcadia editor Jeff Ruetsche, publisher John Pearson, and Sales Director Kate Everingham. They let me call my own game. The hits, the runs . . . the errors—they are all mine. You can't do history on this scale without making a few errors. They are part of baseball and they are part of the publishing game, too.

The following people are also part of this book: Dick Adams, Don Anderson, Lenny Arevalo, Mel Atwell, Irene Ballwey, Helen Baros, Dick and Alice Bartley, Ernie Beck, George Bergmeister, Dick Beverage, Larry Beyersdorf, Bruce Binkowski, Lefty Blason, Ernie Bonn, Ray Brandes, Bob Breitbard, Terry Bertolino, Bill Burdick, Priscilla Burge, Ruby Caldwell, Billy Capps, Andy Castagnola, Bob Cluck, Rick Crawford, John Daly, Sara Davis, Eddie Deal, Rick Diaz, Dick Dobbins, Bob Dreher, John Drehner, Augie Escamilla, Bruce Ericcson, Dave Eskenazi, Ed Fletcher, Jeff Frank, King Freeman, Mick Gammon, Pete Grijalva, Charlie Grimm, Jack Hacker, Rusty Hansen, Brian Hartley, Larry and Tina Hernandez, Al and Pati Hogan, Jack Innis, Chris Jenkins, Emily Jenkins, Rua Johnson, Pat Jones, Stacy Jordan, Margaret Kazmer, Jane Kenealy, Autumn (Durst) and Bud Keltner, Frank Kern, Kevin Kernan, Al Kidd, Kirk Kinney, Bill Kinsella, Philip, Melville and Dave Klauber, Ann Knight, Tom Larwin, Fred Lewis, Ed Linn, Larry Littlefield, Sister Dominica LoBianco, Alan and Norman Lubke, Mark Macrae, Jerry Magee, Tom Maggard, Paul Maracin, Doc Mattei, Vonn Marie May, Walter McCoy, Johnny McDonald, Ginger McMillan, Ron Mikkelson, Chris Milnes, Pete Morrow, Derek Moses, Bob Moss, Joe Naiman, Kevin Nelson, Rich Nelson, Norma Nunez, Susan Painter, John Panter, Nelson Papucci, Fred Peltz, David Porter, Seymour Prell, Chuck Primeau, Heather Ray, Dion Rich, Herm Reich, Frank Rossman, Ed Sanclemente, Elizabeth Schlappi, Chris Schuehle, Jane Selvar, Cyndi Shatzer, Tom Sheridan, Bob Shumake, Steve Sloan, Bob Smith, Jim Smith, Rick Smith, Vern Smith, Bob Sterling, Muriel Strickland, Norm and Leuella Syler, Pete Tapia, Ron Taylor, Marie Templeton, Ralph Thompson, Todd Tobias, Chris Travers, Glenn Turgeon, Frank Valasco, Donna Van Ert, John Wadas, Traci Wagnon, Tad Wildrick, Max West, Gaylon White, Phil White, Carl Wickham, Dennis Wills, Skip Wills, and Earl Wilson, Sr. and Jr.

Dearest Sister,
I did not have time to write you a short letter, so I wrote a long one.
                                        –Blaise Pascal, French mathematician and philosopher

Note to Pascal's sis:
You'll never know how tough it is to write a short book. It's a blivet!
–Bill Swank, American science fair winner and baseball historian

INTRODUCTION

This little book is a road map and photo album of my two-year microfilm journey through the San Diego Central Library, San Diego Historical Society, and San Diego State University Library to discover the roots of our national pastime in San Diego. Have you ever driven across Nevada or Texas . . . or perhaps the moon? Repetitive hours and stark miles of verbiage and boredom blur before your eyes. Suddenly you stumble upon a lost or forgotten player, a team or humorous anecdote. Push the print button to make it real. Cut and paste. Laminate the pages that will trace the odyssey from Horton Plaza to lower Broadway, a distance measured by nine city blocks or seven decades depending on the route you choose. Over three thousand newspaper articles in five scrapbooks are now part of the San Diego Historical Society collection. You are invited to visit the Historical Society Archives to take your own baseball journey. Then you will understand how difficult it was to boil down 66 years of ancient "base ball" and stuff it into 128 pages.

My good friend, Wade Cline, a talented painter, an old Sacramento Solons fan and a curmudgeon, eliminated several paragraphs of text from my tome with a single word written in red pencil: "boring." The early history of base ball in San Diego is, at best, uneven and, at times, well, boring. There is a fine line between thorough and pedantic. But like the game itself, surprise and drama wait in every chapter of this seven-inning trip. Sometimes it may seem too long between pitches or there isn't enough scoring. I have tried to take a lighthearted approach because this isn't rocket science, brain surgery or even theology, though some fools think otherwise. Let's face it—you can't hit a home run every time you step into the batter's box.

When I was initially asked to do a book for Arcadia, they wanted a pictorial history of the Padres from Lane Field to the opening of new Petco Park. I wanted to do the history of baseball in San Diego *before* the Padres. We compromised. I got talked into doing two books. Back in 1995, people at the Historical Society began calling me a baseball historian. I'd never even heard of the term before and felt a little embarrassed and presumptuous to tell people that I was a historian. On the other hand, it did sound better than to say, "I'm retired." With this book, I have finally earned the title.

Have you noticed that "base ball" used to be two words? It remained that way in the *Official Baseball Guide* until 1942. Incidentally, all the photographs used in this book from the Historical Society are for sale. Several of the other photos are from another Balboa Park treasure, the San Diego Hall of Champions. Many friends and historical societies generously shared their pictures to complete this project.

I estimate that half the people who get this book will only look at the pictures and turn the pages. While this provides a good thumbnail sketch of early base ball in San Diego, the photos and captions at the end of each chapter do greatly enhance the text. If some are overwhelmed with too much amateur baseball in the later chapters, they may be tempted to skip to the end of the chapter for the pictorial history of that decade.

Hopefully this book will inspire a budding historian to follow-up on the major impact of black baseball in San Diego . . . or a SABR nerd to compile the statistics of the ill-fated 1913 Southern California League or 1929 California State League . . . or an ordinary fan simply to pursue research on players and teams from the early years. Did you know that Hall of Famers Rube Waddell, Walter Johnson, Ty Cobb, Grover Cleveland Alexander, and Satchel Paige all played *for* San Diego teams prior to 1936. Babe Ruth, Lou Gehrig, Jimmie Foxx, Al Simmons, and Casey Stengel barnstormed in San Diego. Rube Foster's "Colored" Chicago American Giants practically lived in San Diego during 1913.

As this story unfolded, the concept of revenue became as important as a solid line drive or unhittable fast ball. Sandlot games and leagues may have been exciting at the time, but today they are footnotes. I may have included too much information about them, but often they were the only game in town. It was professional baseball that titillated, frustrated and captured the imagination of the fans. Credit is given to the early local promoters who were pivotal and essential to the success of baseball in San Diego. None got rich for their efforts. They just hoped to break even, but profit was always their motive. They learned the hard way that San Diegans have always been reluctant to support a loser. Sometimes they wouldn't even support a winner.

On a personal level, we do not always know when we may walk in the footprints of history. My family moved to San Diego in 1955. My mother worked as a maid at the Rancho 101 Motel on Pacific Highway which was located on the present site of Mossy Ford in Pacific Beach. My after-school job was to sweep the halls, walkways and parking lot at the "101." While doing research on this project, I discovered that the Driving Park Horse Race Track in PB was a popular base ball venue during the late nineteenth century. To my surprise, the tower at Rancho 101 was the only vestige of the old ballpark. I remember washing the outside windows on that tower. How many times did I also unknowingly sweep home plate?

The sun was shining brightly. The mercury, as usual, was locked in at 72 degrees. This is old-time base ball in San Diego.

This is a typical page from one of the five research scrapbooks used to write this book.

THE OLD BALLPARK. There are no known photographs of Driving Park Race Track in Pacific Beach. The park and grandstands were also used for base ball from 1887 through 1889. This picture of the backside of the judge's stand was taken in 1935. Note the horse atop the weather vane. (Courtesy San Diego Historical Society, SDHS #15619)

THE FIRST PRO GUESTS. The tower was a guest suite at the Rancho 101 Motel shown in this 1955 photograph. The motel was razed in 1968 to make way for the Mossy Ford dealership on East Mission Bay Drive. Back in 1887, George Wright (left) brought his Philadelphia Phillies to play the San Diegos at Driving Park. It was the first professional baseball game in San Diego. (Courtesy of Pacific Beach Historical Society.)

THE AUTHOR. Bill Swank (left, above and below) is San Diego's Baseball Santa Claus. Visit him at the Spreckels Organ Pavilion in Balboa Park during "Christmas on the Prado." In 2003, Santa played second base for the original House of David vintage base ball team in Geneva, Illinois. He successfully executed the old hidden-ball-in-the-beard trick taught to him by legendary HOD catcher, 98-year old Eddie Deal. (Photo below courtesy Eileen Lapins)

ONE

"A Gentleman Asks. . ."

1870–1879

San Diego Population: 2,300
Weather: Sunny, 72 degrees

San Diego's first newspaper, the *San Diego Herald*, debuted on May 29, 1851. Sports coverage was sparse in those days. There was nothing to report. Billiards, bowling and boredom helped pass the time in the sleepy watering holes of Old San Diego. There were occasional rifle and pistol matches or "exciting Indian sack races" to mark the holidays. In 1856, an impromptu three and a half-mile race between a mule team and a pair of plugs ended in a thrilling "three quarters of an inch" victory for the nags. The mules would have won, but they were delayed for a half hour by "the little doctor falling over the tail board of the wagon." Such trauma was commonplace in Southern California even before the advent of the automobile, freeway pileups and road rage. Otherwise, San Diego was a pretty laid back kind of place. Dullsville might have been a better description.

On September 7, 1870, a glimmer of hope finally appeared in the *San Diego Union*: "BASE BALL—A gentleman asks whether there is such an institution as a base ball club in San Diego. He thinks there are active young men enough here to put the thing through. We haven't any club here now, but, as he says, there are men enough, and there is plenty of room."

Nothing happened.

Almost a year later, in May of 1871, a local merchant named Daniel Ullman announced efforts to organize a base ball club. Before teams could even be formed, 18 eager ballists met on the Sixth of May on the Plaza in New Town, which was located directly south of the newly constructed Horton House Hotel (the current downtown sites of Horton Plaza and the U.S. Grant Hotel). It was the first recorded game of base ball in San Diego. The results of this contest are lost to the ages, but base ball fever would infect the tiny border town.

The *Union* boldly predicted that in a short time, San Diego "would compete credibly with the best clubs in California." Note was made of the city's fine climate that should make base ball a "favorite game." To keep things in perspective, that same day, troops from the 1st Cavalry arrived from Fort Yuma and boarded a steamer bound for San Francisco after "service against the Apaches" in Arizona.

The newspaper boast was outrageous indeed. Base ball had already been played in the Golden State for over 20 years. Alexander Joy Cartwright, Jr., the father of modern base ball, has long been credited with introducing the sport to California in 1849. Supposedly in the brief span of five days during a San Francisco stopover while en route to Hawaii, he encountered a few 49ers who were more interested in playing in the outfield than in the gold fields. And, baseball was invented in Cooperstown, too.

Apparently it took 10 years before teams were "officially" organized to play the first recognized game of base ball in 1859. According to an article in an 1851 issue of *Alta* newspaper, "A game of base ball was played upon the [San Francisco] Plaza yesterday afternoon by a number of the sporting gentlemen about town." According to baseball prehistorian Angus Macfarlane, it is quite possible that soldiers from the First New York Volunteers, scattered throughout San Francisco, Sonoma, Monterey, and Santa Barbara during the Mexican War, introduced the game to California as early as 1847.

The transcontinental railroad was completed in 1869, the same year the Cincinnati Red Stockings became base ball's first professional team. To cover expenses, the Reds organized a coast-to-coast tour to take on all comers. Their undefeated year-long trek resulted in 57 victories. The Red Stockings played six games against San Francisco clubs and won them convincingly: 35-4, 58-4, 66-4, 54-5, 76-5, and 46-14. For those keeping score at home, that is a cumulative 335 to 36 rout. The Friscos had a long way to go to catch Cincinnati. It would still be another two years before the first game of base ball was even played in San Diego.

While Mr. Ullman was busy organizing his New Town team, Old San Diego issued a challenge. The clubs met on May 27, 1871, at an unknown venue with ominous results for Extempore of Old Town. Their team name, Extempore, means "without preparation." Old Town played without preparation, without a centerfielder, and without a right fielder. In a surprisingly close game, Ullman's crew prevailed, 48-35.

The teams agreed to a Fourth of July rematch. La Playa (Point Loma) was suggested as "the proper place to play the match." Spectators could sail aboard the *Vaquero* to watch the game and enjoy the beach. This would have been the nineteenth century equivalent of parking your car at Qualcomm Stadium and taking the trolley to Petco. San Diego had three distinct communities in the 1870s: Old San Diego, New San Diego, and La Playa (Pt. Loma). The combined population of these settlements was approximately 2,300. The game could have been played in any of them.

The first local box score appeared in the July 6, 1872 issue of the *San Diego Union*. Outs and runs are shown above the line score and "Fly catches" are at the bottom. According to the 1860 *First Rules of Base Ball*, "A ball being struck or tipped, and caught either flying or on the first bound, is a hand out." Gloves were rarely used, so it was a special fielder who could catch a ball on the fly rather than waiting for the first bounce.

Ullman's New Town Lone Star team again faced the undermanned Old Towners with ominous results for the later club. Ullman, a good sport and fine gentleman, agreed to play with the Old Town "Desperates" (without hope). They were destroyed this time, 51-8. In the 1870s, three things were required to play our national pastime: a ball, a bat, and good sportsmanship. A sense of humor also came in handy.

Other early teams including Young America BBC were formed and "matches" were held around town. Little else is known about the early ballist clubs, but Old Town, where Father Serra planted his crossed bats in 1769, finished the first season of base ball in last place. Perhaps their nickname should have been the Padres.

On March 16, 1872, the Young Eagle Club of New Town outscored the Young Americans of Old San Diego by 15 runs. Later, on December 21, the Young Eagles crushed Rockford of Old Town, 49-14, at the public school grounds, south of B Street between Sixth and Seventh. Henry Brandt scored nine times for the Eagles that day. E. Gregg and Samuel Grieson each had a "fly catch" for the victors.

Other base ball matches were played that year, but sports coverage was buried beside snake oil advertisements, hotel registrations, ship movements, real estate speculation, agriculture reports, crime vignettes, church business, and petty gossip. During the 1870s, San Diego was better known for honey than home runs. By 1875, county bees led the state league in honey production. The newspaper carried more stories about beekeepers than ball players.

The top clubs in 1873 were Coronada and Loma. Several of the original San Diego ballists including Choate, Butrick, Russell, Gregg, and Parsons played for these teams. On June 19, Coronada defeated Loma, 29-21. The teams met again on the Fourth of July at the race track in Old San Diego. The Lomas edged Coronada, 18-17. The championship game was not held until January 1, 1874, on the grounds south of the public school house. The Coronadas defeated the Lomas, 56-37. Do not necessarily be misled by the high scores. A good pitcher would toss the ball exactly where the batter wanted it. It was easier to hit a ball than it was to catch it.

This item appeared on October 4, 1874, in the *Daily Union*:

BASE BALL. The San Diego "Nine" have received a rather fear-inspiring challenge from the Los Angeles Base Ball Club to play a match game as soon as possible. We are assured that there is not the slightest possibility of its being accepted. The Nines' "muscle" is not large enough yet to warrant them attacking such a prodigy as this Club seems to be. However, thinking that the description of the players which accompanied the challenge may prove of interest to our readers, we give this extract:

"In order to keep up the regulation of Base Ball in this city, I have organized a club of which we may well be proud. My pitcher has been practicing for several weeks, and though not in the best of spirits, can now throw a ball with such swiftness that it cannot be seen unless covered with phosphorus, and often the friction caused by its passing through the air produces heat enough to burn the ball to ashes, so that the astonished catcher finds nothing in his hands but a mass of cinders. The catcher has been engaged in breaking pig iron in the foundry; to still farther toughen his hands he allows a two hundred ton trip hammer to fall on them twelve hours a day. They are about the size of a windmill, and if the ball gets by them it will be by traversing the atmosphere of an adjoining county.

My first baseman is trying the diet system to steady his nerves, and can let a government mule kick him in the abdomen all day without wincing. He will never move his foot from the sand bag unless in the way of duty, and a runner for first may light on him like a night-hawk on a flea, but still he stands as immovable as a rock.

My second baseman has devoted himself more especially for active service. He can stand on his head, catch a ball with his feet, reverse his position, knock a grasshopper off a malvern stock, or any other stock.

The third baseman has been making sour-kraut and riding a velocipede to develop the muscles in his lower limbs which are immense and give him the appearance of being troubled with Elephantiasis.

Short stop is probably the best man at his position that can be found this side of the Suez Canal. He is short himself, and has been living on piecrust for six months.

My three fielders have been frisking about the country all the past Summer, drinking angle worm oil to give suppleness to their limbs. They can go on all fours faster than Dexter or Goldsmith Maid can trot, and are so limber that circus men die off like sheep after seeing them perform."

No; we rather guess that challenge won't be accepted immediately.

A "capital match" was scheduled for "the old ball grounds opposite the school houses" on

Thanksgiving Day. Sides would be chosen at game time. As usual, "the ladies especially" were invited to attend. There is no record of how many ladies were in the crowd, but the turnout was said to be good. Two nines were selected. The Bon Tons beat the Dolly Vardens, 37-22.

"The biggest game of base ball [Pacifics vs. Eckfords] that has ever been played in this end of the state" was set for Christmas Day, 1874. Seats would be provided for "ladies, who are cordially invited to attend and stimulate by their presence the aspirants to base ball honors to do their level best on this occasion." Two days later, the *Union* reported that the championship match was a "close contest, ending in favor of the 'Eckfords'. We have not been favored with the score, but are satisfied that the boys did their level best."

Across the nation, base ball had become an integral part of holiday celebrations, but the national pastime had disappeared locally. The Fourth of July in 1876 was to be the biggest party ever held in San Diego ... the Centennial Anniversary of the United States of America. San Diego planned a grand parade, patriotic speeches, a sumptuous banquet, but no base ball match. A few days later, *Union* readers were getting the first telegraphic accounts that "Gen. Custar's (sic) command annihilated" at Little Big Horn in Montana Territory.

Base ball was not mentioned again for three years. On December 23, 1877, an open invitation was extended for all citizens to participate in a Christmas Day game. Results were never given and perhaps the game was not even played. Other news of the day included a story about a "marriage festival" for Kate Sykes and Augustus Cravath.

Almost a year later, on September 8, 1878, out of left field (which was not a cliche in those days), Mr. S.E. Patton, captain of the Resolute B.B.C., issued a strongly worded challenge and $20 wager to any "baseball" (one word) club in San Diego. This drew the attention of prominent businessman George Marston and the Bay City Base Ball Club. As a harbinger of the modern game, the *Union* reported on all of the posturing, bragging, and whining.

A date was selected for these juggernauts to meet on September 28 at Lockling Square (the vacant lot bordered by C and D Streets, Sixth and Seventh Avenues.) Both clubs agreed that a game was played, but Bay City dismissed the Resolutes' "easy victory" over a "picked nine" because two of their players were "absent and three disabled." The Resolute BBC countered that "an erroneous impression [had been] conveyed" and "we feel confident that the majority of the Bay Citys were not accessory to the thin subterfuge." They claimed the correct and final score was 49 to 11 in their favor

"Nine Defeated Base Ballists" fired back that "the Great Mogul of the 'Resolutes' *certainly does* convey an erroneous impression." The nine decided to play a "friendly contest ... not wishing to disappoint the 'Resolutes' and a generous public." The Bay Boys did not want the game to count, but, for the sake of argument, let's give the win to the Resolutes. We know that, on October 5, they also won the second game, 22-19. The Resolutes would be up, 2-0.

The *Union* reported on October 15, 1878, "OUR base ball clubs are nerving themselves in a mighty effort on Saturday afternoon next, when the biggest kind of game is to be played."

Bay City easily won the third game by 17 runs. The club enjoyed an oyster supper provided by a team member "in memory of the victory." Bay City won game four, 10-7, described as, "undoubtedly the best game ever played in the county." The series was tied. "The largest number of ladies and gentlemen" attended the November 2 game. Bay City was on a roll. They won, 23-10, and led the competition three games to two.

A week later, the Resolutes bounced back to defeat "a picked nine," 18-16. Was this actually a reconstituted Bay City team? Would there be more controversy? It appears the series was considered even because the two teams met for one final game on November 16, 1878. The Resolute club came from behind in the seventh inning to beat Bay City, 21-11, in a game "witnessed by the usual large crowd of spectators." The Resolutes were declared the true champions, but, more importantly, base ball was again alive in San Diego.

The rivals joined forces and invited the Academy Base Ball Club of Los Angeles to San Diego for a three-game Thanksgiving set. The Angeles team sailed into town aboard the steamer *Orizaba*. The first game before "several hundred ladies and gentlemen" was a seesaw battle until the seventh when San Diego put eight runs across the plate to claim victory, 29-24. Because the visitors provided a "lively ball," Academy pounded out 34 hits while the San Diegos collected 30 safeties.

San Diego easily won the second game, 34-9, and the last match was held on Thanksgiving Day. The crowd for the finale was estimated between five and six hundred. In the opinion of the home team, Los Angeles made several misinterpretations of the rules. Being gracious hosts (and enjoying a comfortable lead), San Diego willingly gave "every doubt to their opponents." The final score was 35-14. San Diego had 43 hits in each of the last two games to sweep Los Angeles, 3-0. Beating LA has always been sweet for San Diego fans.

Following the contest, "the base ballists repaired to the Horton House where an elegant Thanksgiving dinner awaited them. Toasts were given, songs were sung, and wit and humor abounded." The Academy team was escorted to the steamer *Apcon* by their new friends who sent them home "with three hearty cheers and a tiger." (A tiger is a growl.)

Letters of inquiry were sent to Henry Chadwick (editor of the *New York Clipper*), Albert Spalding (founder of Spalding & Brothers Sporting Goods), and George Wright (captain of the National League Champion Boston Base Ball Club) to ask if umpire Will M. Smith made a correct rule interpretation in the Thanksgiving game. A San Diego runner ran past first base and continued to second when the opportunity presented. Los Angeles complained that the runner had to re-tag first base before proceeding to second on the play. Smith allowed the runner to remain on second base until the Los Angeles club threatened to walk of the field. All three experts replied that the umpire's decision was correct. Wright, the new manager of the Providence Base Ball Club, suggested that if his team won the championship, he would bring it to San Diego at the end of the 1879 season. John Montgomery Ward posted 47 victories on the mound and Providence took the National League crown, but they did not make the trip to San Diego.

Remarkably, base ball was not mentioned again in the *Union* until Thanksgiving 1879. The Coronada BBC hosted a Ball at the Horton House the night before their championship game with San Diego. "The gay colors of the uniforms of the Club formed a very pleasing feature of the evening." The overly-confident Coronada boys danced and drank right up to game time. Although a score was not given for the Thanksgiving match, suffice to say that Coronada lost. They, of course, blamed their downfall on too much dancing.

A couple of "junior clubs" also played on Thanksgiving Day. The Stars smashed the Little Buttercups, 25-19.

On December 6, 1879, a sober and determined Coronada nine bested San Diego, 32-21. Mr. Palmer of San Diego walked around the bases on a smash that was hit so hard the fielders were unable to find the ball. In the meantime, "pedestrianism" had become popular at Locking Square where a walking course was laid out around the ball grounds. More people were walking than playing baseball.

THE PLAZA. On May 6, 1871, 18 eager ballists played a pick-up game on the Plaza in New Town (located directly south of the newly constructed Horton House Hotel on the current site of Horton Plaza and the U.S. Grant Hotel). It was the first recorded game of base ball in San Diego. (Courtesy San Diego Historical Society, SDHS #80:5933)

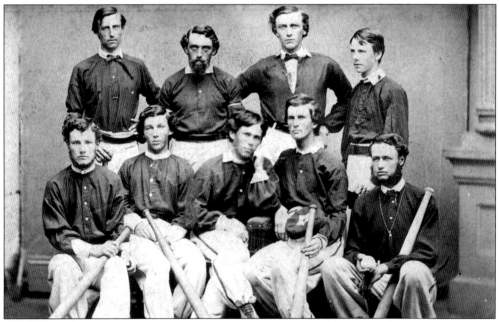

BELOIT COLLEGE BASE BALL TEAM. Nineteen-year-old George Marston (back row, far right) was a skinny right fielder for the Beloit College Olympians base ball team in Wisconsin in 1869. The following year, he moved to San Diego. Marston's first job was as a clerk at the Horton House. A true crank (fan), he could have been one of the eighteen young men to play in the first Plaza game. In 1878, Marston helped establish the well-dressed and well-mannered Bay City Base Ball Club. His influence on the local game diminished in the 1880s, because Mr. Marston, a civic leader and philanthropist, was opposed to base ball on the Sabbath. (Courtesy San Diego Historical Society, SDHS #10116)

Coronadas vs. Lomas, 1873 Championship Game. The top two clubs of 1873 were Coronada and Loma. A championship game was played on January 1, 1874, on the grounds south of the public school house. The Coronadas defeated the Lomas, 56-37. (Courtesy San Diego Historical Society, SDHS #3627)

New San Diego. This 1870s view of New Town, with San Diego Bay and Coronado in the background, shows the location of the early downtown diamonds. The Plaza was south of "D" Street (Broadway) between Third and Fourth Avenues. The Public School Grounds and Lockling Square were north of "D" Street between Sixth and Seventh Avenues. (Courtesy San Diego Historical Society, SDHS #80:2817)

The Base Ball Match. — The base ball match which was played on the afternoon of the fourth of July, between the "Lone Star" Club and the "Old San Diego" Club, resulted in a victory for the first named Club. The game was witnessed by a number of spectators. The Score is as follows:

Lone Star	O.	R.	Old San Diego	O.	R.
Courtney, r f	3.	7	Ullman, 2 b	3.	2
A. Gregg, c	5.	3	A. Aguerro, 1 b	3.	2
Russell, 1 b	1.	9	Collins, s s	2.	2
Butrick, 2 b	3.	6	Hayes, 3 b	2.	1
W. Gregg, s s	1.	6	M. Aguerre, l f	5.	0
Grant, l f	6.	4	Choate, c	4.	0
McKean, p	1.	6	Donahue, p	3.	0
Parsons, c f	3.	5	Smith, r f	3.	0
Harris, 3 b	4.	5	Eaton, c f	2.	1

Lone Star – 2, 1, 8, 8, 0, 9, 7, 9, 7–51.
Old San Diego – 2, 0, 0, 0, 4, 2, 0, 0, 0–8.

Umpire– Mr. Spencer. Scorers–For the "Lone Star," N. C. Maher; for the "Old San Diego," E. O. Wheeler. Fly Catches, "Lone Star" 6; "Old San Diego," 8.

𝕾𝖆𝖓 𝕯𝖎𝖊𝖌𝖔 𝖀𝖓𝖎𝖔𝖓, Dec 22, 1878

Boston, Mass., Dec. 10- O.S. Hubbell, Esq., - Dear Sir: Your letter received, and in answer to your question would state that the decision as given was right. The runner had the right to go to second base without returning to touch first base, providing he touched the same in running over it.

I notice that base ball has taken quite a start out your way. I was thinking, if I could make satisfactory arrangements, I would like to visit your state next Fall, in company with my Club, the Providence," providing they first prove successful in their contest for the championship next season on this way. Providence has one of the strongest nines, organized to battle for the championship, and unless they should gain the title I would not care to go; but it is only time that will tell that. If you think well of it, my Club would be pleased to hear from you at any time. I am, yours truly,
GEO. WRIGHT
Captain Providence B.B.C.

left: FIRST BOX SCORE, SAN DIEGO UNION, JULY 6, 1872. *right:* LETTER FROM GEORGE WRIGHT.

S.S. ORIZABA. Since San Diego did not have railroad service, ball clubs traveled to and from Los Angeles by steamship. (Courtesy San Diego Historical Society, SDHS #80:7658)

TWO

"Games were Jocund and
Joyous"

1880–1889

San Diego Population: 2,637
Weather: Sunny, 72 degrees

A cautionary letter signed "Base Ballist" appeared in the *Union* on June 26, 1880. A championship series was scheduled against a visiting team that was "considered good." The ballist scolded the San Diego lads and implored them to "practice more regularly." Their opposition would be the Orange Base Ball Club. The flowery, convoluted inning-by-inning coverage of the games which appeared in the newspaper was both unprecedented and unintelligible:

> Gansey (the Orange left fielder) took the ash and pending a brief delay occasioned by a loose base, a beautiful 'Mocking Bird' in full plumage perched on the instruments of the Band, who rendered that popular air in their happiest style, leaving nothing better to be desired. A badly thrown ball, poorly caught, secured Gansey his first base, going to second and third as opportunity offered. Boss went out on three strikes, when Capt. Parker was again called, who sent up a star-hunter which came down a foul, and went out on another sky-searcher which went up perpendicularly over the home base, coming down into the extended digits of the committee of one who went to retrieve it. Tally—first big 'O' for the Orange.

Huh? San Diego won the opener, 4-1, and "the game was one of the most brilliant perhaps ever played on the coast, being rarely equaled by the most noted professionals of the East." San Diego took the second game, 7-3. "Nothing whatever occurred throughout the play to mar the good feelings which have existed between the two clubs from the start."

According to Henry Schwartz, Alonzo Horton was present at one of the games. The Father of San Diego always wore a "dark suit with long, formal coat, topped by a tall silk hat."

Apparently a foul ball "alighted on Mr. A.E. Horton's head. Never one to be nonplused, Horton demanded San Diego be given a score based on his miraculous catch. The umpire refused, and the crowd burst out laughing."

The Orange fans pitched a cozy camp at Seventh and D (Broadway) during their three-day stay. Their ladies were described as "pleasant and agreeable acquaintances." The San Diegos swept the series with a 5-4 victory in the final game. An unusual three game box score was published so others throughout the state could see "that three more brilliant games have seldom been witnessed."

Mr. W.C. Travis, secretary of the Orange BBC sent a card to the paper complimenting the "cordial and gentlemanly reception accorded them." He politely thanked the San Diego "ladies for their beautiful bouquets; to the Band for their fine music at the ball grounds ... and to the public in general for their friendly and hospitable treatment."

Later that year, San Diego was invited to participate in an important tournament at the Los Angeles Horticulture Fair. A warm-up game was scheduled with Brayton, the local Army club. The soldiers wore their new red and white uniforms. "Commissary" Carolan smashed the only home run recorded in San Diego that year. The Army third baseman hit a "long-range rifle-ball down through the centre field, across all the intervening ditches and landing the same away below D (Broadway) Street." It mattered little. After dispatching Brayton, 16-5, the San Diegos were ready for tournament play.

The San Diego Base Ball Club sailed to Los Angeles aboard the *Orizaba* on October 18, 1880. Their first game was against Acme, a reorganized version of Academy, the same team San Diego had dominated in 1878. The Los Angles club paid half the expenses to reciprocate for the courtesies extended two years earlier. On October 21, The *Los Angles Herald* reported that the Acme club "played miserably and were unmercifully beaten" by SDBBC, 15-2. San Diego became the favorite and would face the same Orange team they had squeezed three times earlier in the summer.

The next day, Orange took both ends of a doubleheader from San Diego, 16-8 and 20-8. The *Herald* praised the courage and play of Orange catcher Jesse Travis. The San Diego boys complained in the *Union* that Travis "went back on them." The rules of the day stated that any ball caught on one bounce, including a foul to the catcher, was an out. Apparently Mr. Travis had learned a new trick since August.

San Diego sailed home with a "prize" on October 23, following an apparent narrow victory over Acme, 15-14. The Los Angeles newspaper saw it differently: ". . . the game resulted in a tie, each club making 15 runs." We prefer the *Union's* account.

After a successful year, all local club members were invited to meet at the Recreation Grounds on New Years Day 1881 for a game of base ball. The results are unknown and this was the last thing written about base ball in 1881. Christmas was an unusually quiet affair in San Diego that year. "There was a conspicuous absence of material for locals. Little or no business was transacted, there were no accidents, no drunks, no fights. [And no base ball either] Peace and good cheer were the order of the day." So wrote the *San Diego Union* on December 27, 1881.

During a January base ball game at Mrs. Bush's school on "F" Street, a ball went through "a large pane of glass in a window" at Dr. Remondino's home. The replacement cost would be "about two dollars." The 18 playmates of the boy who threw the ball into the doctor's parlor each chipped in ten cents. A *San Diego Union* article proudly stated, "That was the proper way to look at it, boys, and we give you credit for your quick perception of the equity of the case. There are many grown people who would have applied the 'letter of the law,' and 'shirked all responsibility'."

On July 4, 1882, Riverside outscored San Diego, 26-8. The *Union* wrote, "But don't imagine that San Diego can always be beaten so easily. There are some scientific players here." For you non-scientists, scientific base ball involved clever strategies to manufacture runs and intricate statistical analysis to measure player performance.

Although the local base ball club got new uniforms and made "a nobby [stylish] appearance," they stopped playing the game. On October 20, 1883, the *Union* reported that, "The time of the youth of our city is now divided between football and skating." What happened to base ball in San Diego? On February 23, 1884, a *Union* article concluded with, "The National game has not been played in this city for over two years. Let the boys wake up and indulge occasionally in athletic exercise. Don't all be dudes."

In 1882, Russ School opened near Twelfth Street on the southern frontier of dedicated land, which would eventually become Balboa Park. By 1884, the upstairs grew into a high school. On October 30, 1885, the school boys defeated a team called the "No Goods" by nine runs. The incredible athletic tradition of San Diego High School began with a victory.

Local interest in base ball was renewed in 1886, possibly aided by the formation of the professional California League, which included teams from San Francisco, Oakland and Sacramento. A grand Fourth of July celebration was planned for Coronado Beach. A match game of base ball between the Coronado Nine and Athletic Clubs was to be played at the Peninsula ball grounds. The results are unknown. We do know the San Diego Base Ball Club was soundly defeated by Los Angeles, 23-3.

A game between the Shamrocks and San Diegos at the Army Barracks grounds in October of 1886 provided some extracurricular excitement. One of the catchers and the umpire got into a "scrapping match" when the former "expressed his dissatisfaction in strong language." There was a brief episode of "fisticuffs from which one escaped with a black eye and the other with nearly a broken nose." The Shamrocks won the game, 35-12.

On Washington's Birthday in 1887, the Coronados of San Diego encountered a stronger, heavier National City team in the first of a three-game series for the county championship and an oyster supper. The Nationals took the opener, 17-11, on their home dirt, but the Coronados won the second game, 16-12. The Nationals were guilty of "considerable kicking," but most agreed that Umpire Ashbaugh "distinguished himself by his fairness and ability." It is unclear which club eventually won the championship, but it appears the Coronados enjoyed the oysters.

"Hurrah!" The "most eventful Fourth of July [1887] that this city has ever seen" proclaimed the *San Diego Union*. There would be a grand parade, literary and musical exercises, pageantry, rowing, sailing, shooting, fireworks . . . but no mention of base ball. What a lousy celebration! A couple days later, the *Union* carried a story about amateur players enjoying base ball on the newly reclaimed swamp lands south of the Washington Monument in the District of Columbia. If only San Diego could reclaim a mud flat or two, base ball might have a chance. Three and four-line base ball news snippets occasionally appeared in the *San Diego Union*, but the local game was again flagging.

In the meantime, San Francisco newspaper columnist and satirist Ambrose Bierse created *The Devil's Dictionary* in his own image. His definition for Monday: "*n*. In Christian countries, the day after the base ball game." The first illustration of base ball does not appear in the *San Diego Union* until September 18, 1887. Unfortunately, the accompanying article was about how base ball had "captured" San Francisco. The point was that San Diego had not been "attacked with baseball fever." Also addressed was the hot button issue about "How the Sabbath is desecrated." Could it be there were there too many preachers and not enough sinners in San Diego?

Base ball was actually on the cusp of respectability and popularity with San Diego's leading citizens. The game itself had become a social event and source of civic pride. Fancy uniforms replaced "boiled shirts and starched collars." The sport was finally being featured year around rather than as the occasional underbill for major holidays. Gents liked to pose for tintype photos in stylish ball costumes to impress the ladies.

On November 8, 1887, on a vacant lot at the corner of Fouteenth and N Streets, a pickup team embarrassed the fine gentlemen of San Diego, 18-5. This signaled that the San Diegos were in serious trouble as they made preparation for their biggest challenge ever, a two-game series against the Philadelphia Phillies at Driving Park. This Pacific Beach horse race track was better known for fillies than Phillies in the 1880s. It would serve as San Diego's first true multi-purpose sports venue.

The Phillies arrived in style at the Horton House on the evening of November 14, 1887. A young boy reportedly peered through the hotel window and told "a crowd of urchins: I sees de batt'ry boys; der's Ferge [Charlie Ferguson] and Maguire [Deacon McGuire], an' Jack Stafford is talkin' to 'em. I know 'em, you bet; didn't I use ter see 'em play in 'Delphy?" They were, indeed, the genuine Philadelphia Phillies who had just completed a very successful National League campaign in which they finished second to Detroit.

The Phillies were managed by future Hall of Famer, Harry Wright, known as the "Father of Professional Baseball." In 1869, one hundred years before the Padres went big league, Wright organized baseball's first professional team, the Cincinnati Red Stockings. He immediately took them on the road to face all comers. In 1874, he took another team on a round-the-world tour. In Egypt, more camels than people watched an exhibition. Wright introduced professional base ball to exotic places . . . like San Diego.

Philadelphia pitcher Charlie Ferguson had registered the league's lowest ERA (1.98) the previous year and had won over 20 games during each his four seasons with the Phillies. McGuire, a durable catcher, posted a lifetime .278 batting average in a career that spanned 26 seasons. First baseman Dandy George Wood was one of base ball's early home run kings, and left fielder Jim Fogarty led the National League with 99 stolen bases in 1889. These men could play the game.

"About 300 lovers of the National game" including "a number of ladies" caught the train to PB to witness San Diego commit 17 errors and come out on the short end of the 31-7 score. Errors on the playing field were a common occurrence in 1887 since gloves had not yet come into fashion. The Phillies themselves committed seven errors, but it was the hitting of the Easterners that would dazzle the local cranks (fans) and players.

The following day (November 16), the Phillies again won, 17-1. Considering the skill level of the competition, the San Diego boys acquitted themselves quite well. San Diego first baseman West and pitcher Osburne were singled out for their good play. One of the local boys hit a home run. It must have been West.

Schiller & Murtha Dry Goods Company presented new uniforms to the Acme Baseball Club. The team instantly became the Schiller & Murthas and drew some of San Diego's brightest ballists who were anxious to be seen in the latest fancy duds.

During the winter of 1887–88, the *Union* reported that the San Francisco and Los Angeles teams of the California League held their own with several Eastern teams including the St. Louis Browns, New York Giants, Philadelphia Phillies, and Chicago White Stockings (Cubs). With the start of the 1888 season, base ball stories and standings from the East began to regularly appear on the front page of the *San Diego Union*. Would San Diego soon be joining the California Base Ball League?

A San Diego County championship game was held on May 19, 1888, near Russ School. The San Diego Maroons defeated the Commercial College, 8-3. The college boys had beaten the Shamrocks, 15-10, in April for undisclosed prize money. Apparently, the Maroons were quickly cobbled together from local talent that included several of the top Shamrock players. Other county teams included the San Diegos, Otay, Escondido, Oceanside, National City, the Hotel del Coronado, Horton House, International Hotel, Fifth Street, Courthouse, the Dreadnaughts, the Buckeyes, the Park Club, the Hadley-Logan Baseball Club, and the old Bay City Club. Players frequently switched teams and used assumed names.

San Bernardino was invited to San Diego for a Fourth of July game with a $100 purse. The San Berdo pitcher bragged that San Diego would be unable hit him. In a related story titled "Diamond Dust," a list of offenses and fines was published since ball players were expected to show respect toward the umpire. "You make me sick," would cost a player $10; "You're rotten,"

$15; "Give us a show," $25; said with a snarl, $30.

Additionally, it was reported that the curve ball had been introduced to the West Coast. Note was made that "with fifteen minutes' practice, it is claimed that any one can pitch all the curves."

Los Angeles replaced San Bernardino and a total of three games were played. "At least 2,000 people took the Pacific Beach trains" to watch the first game. The crowd count was probably inflated. LA took the first two games, 11-7 and 13-9. A big $100 game was scheduled for Independence Day. We will never know which side snagged the money because the results were not published. This was usually an indication the locals lost.

A couple of days later, the *Union* carried excerpts from an article that Joel Benton wrote for the *American Magazine*. Mr. Benton took exception to the professional game which was replacing "the hilariously dominating [children's] game of ball. The old-fashioned games were 'jocund' and joyous, and always played for fun." Now "the pitcher with his peculiar tricks makes hitting the ball either rare, accidental or impossible." Benton denounced modern base ball, a game with a 2,000-year history, as a business and a danger . . . and not a sport.

On August 21, 1888, a meeting was held in the courtroom of Justice Boone to organize an association which would play its games at the new ball grounds located on Newton Avenue between Twenty-Fifth and Twenty-Sixth Streets. The plan was to develop a pool of talent that could beat Los Angeles. The National City team promptly refused to play San Diego on the Sabbath. Julian formed a ball team to challenge the top teams of San Diego County. In September, San Diego became part of a larger effort to participate in the Southern California Base Ball League during the winter months.

In an exciting October contest, the San Diego Maroons thumped the Hotel del Coronado nine, 20-16. Following the contest, two gamblers haggled over their wager. It was agreed the matter would be resolved with fists on the beach. The Maroons backer won the fight and took the money.

The San Diego Base Ball Association met in Justice Monroe's courtroom on October 19, 1888. A recommendation was made to acquire and develop a 300 by 400-foot plot of land at Fouteenth and L Streets for another new ball grounds. Hope was high when it was learned that Eddie Lorrigan, star pitcher for Stockton (also known as Mudville), 1888 California League champions, had moved to town. The beloved poem, "Casey at the Bat," had been written earlier that year by *San Francisco Examiner* editor Ernest Thayer. It mentions several of Lorrigan's Mudville teammates (Flynn, Cooney, and Barrows). Unfortunately young Lorrigan had come to San Diego for health reasons. At 23 years of age, he succumbed of tuberculosis in 1889.

On January 20, 1889, the S. White team won the City Championship from Schiller & Murtha by a 19-9 score at Roseville. Tickets were 20 cents which included the boat ride, the game, and a concert that followed. The recognized star of the Whites club was Mr. Calvin Alexander McVey, 39 years of age and an original member of the 1869 Cincinnati Red Stockings. McVey played in the National League from 1876 through 1879 and compiled a .328 lifetime batting average.

The San Diego Base Ball Commercial League replaced the Association in April 1889. All games were scheduled at renovated Driving Park. A heavy canvas backstop replaced the old wooden boards used in the past. The Whites were reorganized as F.N. Hamilton. Their uniforms would be handsome, form-fit maroon jerseys and knickerbockers. The Schiller & Murtha team would also sport new threads. The new Llewelyns club, sponsored by a shoe store, would wear navy blue garments trimmed with white. Unfortunately, the grand parade had to be canceled several times because the uniforms were not aboard the weekly ship arrivals from San Francisco.

By the end of April, the addition of the Otay Watch Factory club filled out a four-team schedule. In their first game, Otay catcher J.E. Shaffer was credited with setting "a new world record" by catching 16 foul tips which were recorded as outs. By the middle of May, because of poor attendance in Pacific Beach, all games were transferred to the ball grounds at Twenty-Fifth and Newton. Plans were drawn for a new ballpark with bleachers ("bleaching boards") in Logan Heights so the "frugal family man can leave his oil can [seat] at home." On June 23, 1889, league manager William M. Averill, the newly anointed "Father of Base Ball in San Diego," enclosed a 300 by 400-foot lot on the street car line between Milton (National Avenue), Logan, Twenty-Third and Twenty-Fourth Streets. It would be called Recreation Park

The famous traveling Thatcher, Primrose & West Minstrel Combination challenged the locals to a base ball game in July of 1889. Othello played first base for the minstrel troupe. Iago performed at shortstop and King Lear was "behind the bat." A $100 prize was offered, but the stunt proved to be "much ado about nothing."

With the growing popularity of the Sunday base ball league, an obtusely veiled and lengthy sermon about the evils of base ball appeared in the July 28, 1889 San *Diego Union and Daily Bee*. The Reverend F.R. Perkins warned that base ball would corrupt the young children of Logan Heights. The "twin demons" of base ball—gambling and drunkenness—result in "desolated homes, commercial dishonesty, theft, blasted lives, and all forms of vice and violence." Sermons could typically be found in the Monday newspaper that were much longer than any stories about base ball.

The San Diego Board of Delegates were called into session on August 12, 1889. The matter of Sunday base ball was addressed by the Committee on Health and Morals. The city attorney advised the board that any ordinance to ban sport on the Sabbath would undoubtedly be found unconstitutional. In an unrelated matter, saloon-keeper G.M. Thornburgh questioned laws that required San Diego saloons to close at 11:00 p.m. and pay a $50 license fee when the Hotel del Coronado was allowed to operate its saloon all night without a license. The matter was referred to the mayor.

S.J. Sills replaced winless Otay in mid-season. Buried in the cellar on the last day of the season (September 23, 1889), Sills finally broke into the win column with a convincing 13-7 triumph over the Llewelyns. Later that day, F.N. Hamilton faced Schiller & Murtha for the city championship. Cal McVey and Sam Dungan formed a fearsome battery for the favored Hamiltons. Although trailing 5-2 in the bottom of the fourth inning, S&M tallied six times to capture the shiny blue and wine-colored satin pennant, which read, "Schiller & Murtha Base Ball Club, Championship 1889." In the final standings, S&M posted a 16-6 record and F.N. Hamilton went 15-7.

Somehow it was the F.N. Hamilton club that played and twice defeated Escondido in October for the county championship. Later that month, a powerful team from Pomona defeated a picked nine in San Diego, 18-4. There were complaints that "the umpire gave the picked nine the ragged end of the rope." The next day in the rain, the Hamiltons scored twice in the bottom of the ninth to defeat Pomona, 12-11. Although F.N. Hamilton was recognized as the class of San Diego, Schiller & Murtha was the champion.

On Thanksgiving Day, Schiller & Murtha beat Pete Lohman's highly-regarded Los Angeles Tuft-Lyons team, 6-3, at Recreation Park. LA stayed over to manhandle the Llewelyns, 15-7. On the third day, the Hamiltons thumped Los Angeles, 11-5. The *Union* reported, "The visitors have a very much higher opinion of the ball players of San Diego than they had last week." The hosts were impressed with Lohman's ability to stay up all night and play ball the next day. Base ball was again alive as San Diego entered the Gay '90s.

SCORE.			
	1st	2d	3d
SAN DIEGO.	Game.	Game.	Game.
	O. R.	O. R.	O. R.
Tynan, catch............	3 0	2 2	3 1
Bradt, 3d base.........	4 0	3 1	2 1
Russell, 2d base........	4 1	4 0	2 1
Hubbell, short stop......	3 0	2 1	2 1
Spencer, right field......	2 2	2 1	3 0
Hermann, pitch........	1 1	1 1	4 0
Parker, 1st base	2 0	2 0	3 0
Murphy, centre field....	2 0	3 0	3 0
Hubon, left field..........	3 0	5 1	2 1
Totals............	24 4	24 7	24 5

	1st	2d	3d
ORANGE.	Game.	Game.	Game.
	O. R.	O. R.	O. R.
Parker, C.E., pitch.......	2 1	2 0	4 0
Travis, J.C., catch........	4 0	3 0	2 0
Travis, W.C., 1st base....	5 0	4 0	3 0
White, 2d base............	3 0	4 1	3 0
Hemphill, 3d base........	2 0	3 2	4 0
Parker, C.H., short stop..	4 0	1 0	2 2
Garnsey, left field.........	3 0	3 0	3 1
Whitney, centre field.....	3 0	4 0	3 1
Scott, right field........	3 0	3 0	3 0
Totals............	27 1	27 3	27 4

FIRST GAME.

Innings-	1 2 3 4 5 6 7 8 9 R
San Diego.................	0 2 1 0 0 1 0 0 --4
Orange......................	1 0 0 0 0 0 0 0 0 1

Time- 1 hour 26 minutes

SECOND GAME.

Innings-	1 2 3 4 5 6 7 8 9 R
San Diego.................	3 1 2 1 0 1 0 0 --7
Orange......................	0 1 0 2 0 0 0 0 0 3

Time- 1 hour 19 minutes

THIRD GAME.

Innings-	1 2 3 4 5 6 7 8 9 R
San Diego.................	3 0 0 0 0 2 0 0 --5
Orange......................	0 0 1 1 0 0 0 0 2 4

Time- 1 hour 15 minutes

THREE-GAME BOX SCORE AND JIM FOGARTY, PHILADELPHIA PHILLIES. On the left is an unusual three-game box score from the *San Diego Union* (July 6, 1880). Jim Fogarty and the Philadelphia Phillies paid a memorable visit to Pacific Beach in 1887. They played a local team in San Diego's first professional base ball game. Guess who won?

BARRACKS DIAMOND

ARMY BARRACKS. After Lockling Square was developed in 1884, the Army Barracks diamond became a popular venue for base ball in the late 1880s. During the remainder of the decade, games were played on several vacant lots in downtown San Diego: "the diamond north of the Horton House," "near the Carleton House," "grounds at the foot of Fourteenth street," "the G-street grounds," "the grounds corner of Fourteenth and L-streets," "the corner of Fourteenth and M-streets," "corner of Fourteenth and N streets," "the Eleventh street grounds," "the corner of Fourth and A streets" and even on the future site of Lane Field at "the foot of D street [Broadway]." (Courtesy San Diego Historical Society, SDHS #89:17182 detail)

SCHILLER & MURTHA, 1887. Members of this early San Diego ball club, pictured from left to right, are (front row) unknown, Starr, Tom Works, and Will Shaw; (middle row) Lenny Hubron, unknown manager, Harry Mertzman; (back row) Gene Donnelly, Billy Mundell, Jake Schiller, F.D. Murtha, Billy Byler or Will Palmer, and Rufus Choate. (Courtesy San Diego Historical Society, SDHS #10521)

SCHILLER & MURTHA, 1887. The ball players, from left to right, are (front row) W. Kaymer, Lenny Hubon, and Tom Works; (middle row) J. Palmer, unknown, manager Jay Jost, and C. Williams; (back row) E. Weiland, S. Allen, K. Smith, and Oscar Palmer. Both of these popular photograph have been dated "1887." If modern fans think players change teams too often, it was impossible to keep track of them in the nineteenth century. Based on the names, it appears the top photo is from the late 1880s and the lower photo from the early 1890s. Schiller & Murtha was the top team in San Diego during that era. (Courtesy San Diego Historical Society, SDHS #14679 detail)

JULIAN BASE BALL TEAM. Seen here, from left to right, are (front row) Luther Bailey and Mr. Powers; (back row) Ray Detrick, Hardy Ford, unknown, Lou Smith, Leland Wellington, Bob Haley, Claude Swycaffer, Rex Detrick, John Campbell, and Roy Stephens. The *San Diego Union* reported that the Julian team was "ready to challenge the next best team in the county." The miners practiced by swinging their axes at gold nuggets. (Courtesy San Diego Historical Society, SDHS #17786-5)

McFADDEN OF EL CAJON. Pt. Loma beat McFaddens in El Cajon, 11-10, on September 9, 1889. These players do not appear to be as refined as the city boys. (Courtesy San Diego Historical Society, SDHS #9633)

CAL MCVEY AND SAMMY DUNGAN. Both of these men played for F.N. Hamilton in 1889. McVey (left) was an original member of base ball's first professional team, the undefeated 1869 Cincinnati Red Stockings. The National League formed in 1876 and he averaged .328 through 1879. "The Colonel" was player-manager his last two years in Cincinnati. Dungan (right) batted .301 during his five-year major league career. He was the leading hitter of the California League and, later, the American (Western) League in 1890, 1899, and 1900.

F.N. HAMILTON TEAM, 1889. The team's mascot, Sullivan, is in front. Behind him, from left to right, are (front row) Domley, Chase, Mundell, Cal McVey, and unknown; (back row) Silvio Blanco, Vincent, Fred Hamilton, Daniels, W.C. Ermek, and Fred Lange. The Hamiltons were San Diego's other top team in the late 1880s. (Courtesy San Diego Historical Society, SDHS # 11844)

THREE

"San Diego Wins Fame"

1890–1899

San Diego Population: 16,159
Weather: Sunny, 72 degrees

The Southern California Base Ball League had become a reality in December of 1889. Local promoters believed San Diego had sufficient talent to fill two teams. Recreation Park would host ball games every weekend as part of a rotating travel schedule. Civic pride exceeded reality. Los Angeles visited San Diego to play four games in January and February of 1890. The teams in Ventura and Riverside quickly disappeared. After all of the anticipation, parades, concerts, speeches and excuses, San Diego found itself without a single victory in a doomed two-team league. Predictably, LA was declared the champion. The *Union* was harsh: "If San Diego proposes to have a base-ball club why should it not have a club which can play base ball?

In March, a two-game series between that same Los Angeles team and the California State League champions, Oakland, was contested in San Diego. The Los Angeles boys destroyed the Oaks, 13-6 and 16-5. The *Union* reported, ". . . the San Diego public are beginning to realize the fact that the old San Diego club was a pretty good team after all." Local teams played regularly for the remained of the year. On May 25, 1890, San Diego beat Anaheim, 4-3, in a game judged "one of the best seen on the San Diego diamond."

Later that year, a wealthy dude came to town with grandiose ideas to revitalize base ball in San Diego. Marco Hellman, owner of the Los Angeles club, would expand the Southern California Winter League to include San Diego, Riverside, San Francisco, Oakland, Sacramento, and Chicago. Yes, Chicago! The northern teams including Chicago and Canadian Geese would spend the winter in Southern California.

The plan was perfect. The brand new San Diego Cable Railway Company would carry passengers in modern comfort to the newly constructed Recreation Ballpark located at the Bluffs in Mission Heights. Local media praised Hellman for "his money and enthusiastic energy" and for bringing "really first-class work on a San Diego diamond."

The newcomer clearly was a hero . . . a rich owner with a new ballpark and a trolley. To raise $25,000 for the success of this venture, Mr. Hellman suggested that "San Diego should show her appreciation by buying twenty per cent of the stock."

Rain delayed the opening of league play until December 13, 1890. The San Diego nine was actually powerful Sacramento of the California League in disguise. They proudly wore "San Diego" across the front of their uniforms and were described as "a fine-looking set of men." "Honest Jack" Sheridan would be the league umpire. According to Hellman, "This will result in giving people the best exhibition of base ball playing ever seen here."

An enthusiastic crowd of "lovers of the game, pretty women, gay turnouts" watched the transplanted Senators take four straight from Los Angeles. "The grand stands and the bleachers were filled with the society people of the city." Attendance exceeded expectations.

On Christmas Day, San Diego edged San Francisco, 11-10. During that game, Frisco outfielder Reuben Levy collided with the left field fence and his head was severely gashed. "He fell like an ox, but recovered and attempted to throw the ball, the blood the while spurting in a crimson stream from his wound. He kept trying to rise, only to fall again, until he was reached by the other fielders, who picked him up and carried him to the ticket office."

Two days later, the public learned that winter baseball in San Diego was in worse shape than poor Levy. The *Union* reported, ". . . the baseball business that went off with flourish of trumpets and every promise of success is in deep trouble." Hellman had cleaned out the ticket office before ballpark owner George Keyes was able to attach the gate. Like the players, he too was getting stiffed. Despite a proposal for one more game with all receipts going to the players, the league immediately collapsed.

Hellman, the snake, was last seen at the Santa Fe depot. "I want a locomotive quick to take me to Los Angeles. Money is no object." This was the biggest ticket ($500) the young clerk had ever written. In record time, "one of the noblest steeds of the iron cavalry of commerce" appeared on the northbound tracks ready to carry the fallen baseball magnate to sanctuary in the City of Angels. But Hellman failed to pick up his ticket. He had already disappeared into the night.

In November of 1891, depending on the news source, Schiller & Murtha won either their fifth consecutive San Diego or Southern California championship. "A beautiful and costly hand-painted silk banner" was displayed at the annual Thanksgiving base ball game.

A few days later, in a game between S&M and the A. Dorseys, "matters were looking corky" when Clarence Vincent, first baseman for the Dorsey club, misread a curve ball which nailed him. The angry Vincent charged the mound and swung his bat at the head of pitcher Kaymer. The Schiller & Murtha hurler ducked, but his throwing arm caught the full force of the bat and he was unable to continue. Vincent was arrested for assault with a deadly weapon. In court, a "penitent" Vincent paid a $30 fine and vowed to quit the game.

The top teams of 1892 were the equally-matched San Diegos and Schiller & Murtha ball clubs. They would play each other every Sunday at Recreation Park. The San Diegos would win one week; Schiller & Murtha would win the next. It became tedious. The game that captured the most coverage that year involved San Diego's leading citizens known as the "Fat Men."

The slogan of their second annual charity game was, "Feed the hungry. Clothe the naked." The results of this July exhibition were "terrible." Ground balls were difficult to "reach under so much avoirdupois." Batting technique was "evidently acquired by sweeping mosquitos off the wall with a broom." The game was mercifully called after five innings because "the teams would probably be there yet." Judge Witherby's side claimed victory, 18-13.

Newsboys sold $9 worth of water which went into the "cork fund." The next day, young men from Florence Hill proposed their own charity game to raise money to buy a new wooden leg for Tommy Scott, a one-legged newsboy. It is assumed the lad was among the boys selling water at Recreation Park. In an unrelated news item, a live pigeon shoot was also scheduled for the ballpark. When is the last time you saw a pigeon shoot at a ball game? How about a paper boy with a wooden leg?

Base ball nearly disappeared from the local scene in 1893. The *Union* carried results from "the Eastern Leagues," but little was written about the sport in San Diego. Schiller & Murtha easily won two games from the Los Angeles Grays in August. A newly-formed club of local young enthusiasts, the Marquardts, were able to hold their own against the aging S&Ms.

Triumph over any Los Angeles team has always been a source of celebration in San Diego. In October 1893, the SD Cactus defeated the LA Roosters in a pair of home and away games. The Cacti and their cranks who traveled by special railway car to Los Angeles were "tendered a merry dance" by their hosts to honor the victory. "The affair was very swell."

"Baseball enthusiasts are jubilant" proclaimed an article about an 1894 Independence Day clash between the Californias of Los Angeles and the San Diego Cactus club. The California team arrived a day early by special steamship to practice at Recreation Park. Both clubs were composed of men with "social standing." The visitors "were very jubilant over the game, and wired to their home papers glowing accounts of it." Los Angeles chopped the Cactus, 11-4. "The Cacti resolved never again to be caught napping."

San Diego base ball fell into deep slumber after a couple of 1894 Thanksgiving Day games (National City vs. San Diego; Russ School vs. B Street School) and a traditional Christmas Day match between the Russ and B Street boys. The only known baseball in 1895 involved a few games in the spring. One was "unusually interesting" and the other between the Los Angeles Admirals and San Diego Army Barracks apparently was not interesting. The Admirals sank the soldiers, 11-6.

Little of anything happened on San Diego's diamonds in 1896, unless you were a fan of the Jamacha Orange and Green team. The Carrots challenged the Cactus in March and, in August, lost to Spring Valley, 5-4. Occidental College defeated the San Diego Cacti on Memorial Day, 18-17. The next day, the San Diegans beat a woeful collection of out-of-towners dubbed "Los Angeles." The only other reference to our national pastime that year was an advertisement for BattleAx chewing tobacco in the *Union*: "You will never know just how good it is until you try it."

San Diego split the first two games of a three game series with LA over the Fourth of July weekend in 1897. Since the results of the rubber match are unknown, one can only assume that Los Angeles snagged the $100 prize money. Also that summer, the Naval Reserves beat a picked nine, 25-12, and "the Poway Good Templars wiped the ground with the San Diego Good Templars," 21-7. Riverside clubbed San Diego, 15-6, on August 1, 1897.

August 8, 1897, was the grand opening of Bay View Park at Twenty-Fifth Street and Newton Avenue. It was described as, "one of the handsomest ball parks in the state," Two bits would cover round trip transportation by electric car and admission to the game. "Best ball games ever played in San Diego" were being reported in the *Union*. Local leagues were forming. The Fat Men were again "Feeding the hungry. Clothing the naked. Thundering around the base paths." Another Southern California League was created in December to play during the winter months. Interest revived when it was announced that San Diego would have two teams, the San Diegos and the Mercantiles. Professional players were actively recruited to fill out the rosters.

Sammy Dungan, now an established National Leaguer, returned to San Diego. Young "Turkey Mike" Donlin joined the newly-formed Mercantiles. In January 1898 warm-up games, the San Diego Parks, "a picked local nine," beat the Los Angles Colored Trilbys twice, 12-5 and 20-15. Manager Jack Dodge praised the black Trilby team, "whose gentlemanly conduct as well as ball-playing ability, is above average."

The headline of a February 7, 1898 *Union* article boasted, "San Diego Wins Fame." The Parks convincingly defeated a "team composed of many of the stars of the National League," 7-2, at Bay View Park. The Baltimore All Americans won three other games against San Diego teams, but the Parks were the first team to hang an "L" on the "eastern leaguers." Top San Diego clubs were again in competition with other Southern California teams, but a formalized league never materialized. Sporadic games were played with local service nines. When teams would venture south from LA, San Diego whipped them.

The year 1899 marked the beginning of a baseball renaissance, of sorts, in paradise. San Diego won a couple of games from Pomona in January, took two more from Los Angeles in February, and claimed a pair of victories against the Santa Anas in March. Ontario was the only team to beat San Diego that month—twice. Azuza was defeated in April. On May 13, 1899, Phoenix, the champions of Arizona Territory, lost to San Diego, 12-9.

As an interesting footnote, it appears serious consideration was given to include the Colored Trilbys in the new Southern California semi-professional league. Ironically, it was San Diego's lopsided 22-3 victory over the Trilbys and not race that convinced promoters that the Negro team would not be competitive. The point was clear that "colored teams" usually played well and, more importantly, drew fans.

The Southern California Baseball League was formed in May. The *Union's* first attempt at a sports page, "The Field of Sport," appeared on June 19, 1899. Coverage included stories about a shooting contest, rowing, football, bicycle racing, tennis, golf, handball, basketball, water polo, boxing, baseball, and track and field. WP Fuller, San Diego's entry in the new Southern California Baseball League, went north to San Bernardino and was defeated, 21-6, but remained atop the standings with a 3-1 record. The *Union* blamed the loss on "the intense torrid heat . . . over 100 in the shade . . . there is little wonder that the San Diego boys wilted and actually played poor ball."

A week later, the "colored mascot" of the Los Angles Merchants explained a 12-0 loss in San Diego. A *Los Angeles Herald* reporter wrote: "Well, boss, I'll tell 'em this; I done see a Chihuahua dog on de bleachers, and dat dog am a powerful hoodoo. I'll tell 'em dat de Chihuahua dog done de business." The Fullers broke a scoreless tie with seven runs in the fourth inning. The Merchants kicked about umpire Sylvester's calls. "Rag-chewing was indulged" until Judge Hendrick left the bleachers to beg the visitors to resume play. LA captain Long Bill Tyler and his teammates "were unmercifully guyed by the loud-voiced young fellows in the bleachers." Tyler lost his temper and yelled back, "I never saw such a lot of flatheads as you are."

By the middle of July, the Fullers and San Bernardino were locked in a first place tie with identical 7-2 records. The *Union* complained about ballpark etiquette: "Rooting may be a nice thing on the bleachers, but when the grandstand is invaded and made to resound with the bellowing of noisy enthusiasts, the feminine portion of the audience is considerably annoyed."

On August 13, 1899, San Diego's first "colored" team, the Young Giants, faced the Models at Bay View Park. The teams were supposed to represent "the best players in town outside the Fuller team." Among San Diego's first black ballplayers were Wilson, Bullets, Hamilton, Hughes, Price, Saunders, Jackson, Townsend, and Taylor. The results of the game are unknown. The Young Giants, later renamed the Coast Giants, competed for years against white teams in San Diego leagues.

On August 21, 1899, the Pauma and Rincon Indians challenged any "American nine" to a match during their fiesta at the Mission San Luis Rey. The challenge was accepted, but neither side could agree on the purse.

In October, San Bernardino was in first place with 16 victories and six losses. The Fullers were in second with a 14-8 record. The two teams met in San Diego on November 5. The score was tied, 5-5, when the captain of San Bernardino disputed the umpire's call on a close play at third base. He removed his team from the field, so umpire LJ Sylvester awarded the game to the Fullers, 9-0. There was a near riot when the visitors left the ball grounds. A group of San Diego boys tagged along and called the San Berdoos "cowards and other names." San Bernardino left fielder Collins hit Cecil Rapier, son of W.H. Rapier, and an angry mob chased him down Logan Avenue to Sixteenth Street. The police gave the ballplayer a bicycle which he peddled to safety. In the meantime, young Rapier filed a complaint and Collins was arrested for battery. Most importantly, when the season ended, San Diego and San Bernardino were deadlocked with identical 17-9 records.

The championship game was held on a neutral site in Los Angeles. The *Union* reported that the San Diego "players seemed scared" and lost, 10-4. "Umpire Wheeler was just in his decisions, and, so no kicks were made."

In other sporting news, on November 30, 1899, the San Diego football team, led by bruising fullback Clifford Cravath, defeated San Bernardino High School, 11-6, at Bay View Park. Cravath, a native of Escondido, would switch to baseball and become San Diego's first major league player.

A four-team commercial league also started in San Diego. The clubs included Ferris & Ferris Drug Store, the Yellow Kids (named after a popular cartoon strip of that era), the Bay Citys, and El Cajon. Another Southern California Baseball League (or series as the league was humbly known) formed because interest was high. The season began with a four team doubleheader at Bay View Park. San Diego beat Los Angeles, 9-5, in the opener, and San Berdoo took the second game, 3-1, over the LA Athletics. San Diego pounded out an exciting 11-10 victory over arch rival San Bernardino in mid-December and rallied for a 9-7 triumph in San Bernardino on New Year's Eve. The San Diegos were leading the league as the century closed.

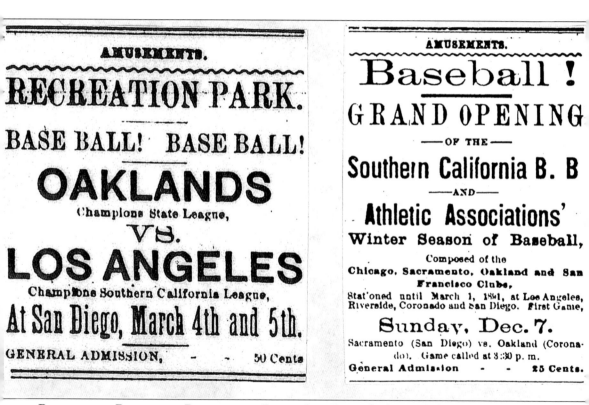

RECREATION PARK AND RECREATION PARK. San Diego had two ballparks known as Recreation Park in the 1890s. The original was accessible by street car at Twenty-Third and Milton Streets (Crosby and National). The newer park, built in 1890, was located at the end of the cable car line on University Avenue (Park Boulevard). To avoid confusion, the diamond at the Bluffs (Mission Cliffs, University Heights) was renamed Athletic Park, which would confuse old-timers when Athletic Park was built at Twenty-Sixth (Sampson) and Newton in 1908. Maybe Qualcomm and Petco aren't so bad after all . . .

SACRAMENTO TEAM, CALIFORNIA LEAGUE, 1890. Local tailors removed S-A-C-R-A-M-E-N-T-O and stitched S-A-N D-I-E-G-O to these uniforms for the 1890 Southern California Winter League season. (Courtesy Haggin Museum, Stockton, California, # 1950.37.4.3)

TAKE A TROLLEY TO THE BALLPARK. San Diego had it all in 1890 . . . a good team, a wealthy owner, a brand new ballpark and a modern trolley line. Then it all fell apart. (Courtesy San Diego Historical Society, SDHS #7775)

"Feed the Hungry. Cloth the Naked." A charity game between San Diego's leading citizens, known as the "Fat Men," received more press coverage than legitimate base ball did in 1892. The mascot (bat boy) was chosen for obvious reasons. (Courtesy San Diego Historical Society, SDHS #99:19923)

Mason Street School. While younger students line up for a class picture, boys impatiently wait to play base ball on the playground of the second Mason Street School in Old San Diego. The original Mason Street School, built in 1865, was San Diego's first public schoolhouse. Notice the other boys shooting marbles on the right. (Courtesy San Diego Historical Society, SDHS #8289)

LA MESA BASE BALL TEAM, 1896. Team members included Charles Walker, Frank Whittier, Ross Osborn, Bick Coal, Roy Williams, Billy Straw, Duane Oliver, Tom Butler, H. Highfield, and "Reamer."

ROMONA AND POWAY BASE BALL TEAMS, 1897. Base ball was more popular in the smaller communities of San Diego County than in the big city during the middle years of the 1890s. Ramona and Poway enjoyed a friendly rivalry. (Courtesy San Diego Historical Society, SDHS #11959)

BAY VIEW PARK, 1897. They couldn't wait for the grandstand to be completed to play base ball inside Bay View Park at Twenty-Fifth (Evans) Street and Newton Avenue in early 1897. (Courtesy San Diego Historical Society, SDHS #89:17438)

COVERED GRANDSTAND, BAY VIEW PARK. The grandstand was finished in August of 1897. (Courtesy San Diego Historical Society, SDHS #22218)

BAY VIEW PARK. The grand opening of Bay View Park was held on August 8, 1897. It was described as, "one of the handsomest ball parks in the state." Colorful signage on the fences reminds old-timers of the way ballparks used to look. (SDHS #22215)

BAY VIEW SPONSOR. The grandstand roof (WP Fuller & Co's. Pure Prepared Paint sign) is visible beyond the outside fence. (Courtesy San Diego Historical Society, SDHS #22219.)

INSIDE THE PARK. This may look like another exterior picture of Bay View Park, but it is actually inside the ballpark. The entire playing surface was dirt. The infield was better groomed, because the bigger rocks were casually thrown as close as possible to the outfield fence. (Courtesy San Diego Historical Society, SDHS #22229)

BAY VIEW TRANSPORTATION. Street car tracks ran along the left field fence. Part of the grandstand can be seen between the pitched roofs. (Courtesy San Diego Historical Society, SDHS #22212)

MERCANTILE TEAM, 1898. These nineteenth century ball players, from left to right, are (front row) unknown, Tom Works, and Jack Hartley; (back row) Gene Williams, Bert Treanor, Charles McDuell, Mr. Crane (owner of the Mercantile Restaurant), Charles VanHorn, Billy Holmquist, and Lew Works. (Courtesy San Diego Historical Society, SDHS #94:19292)

SAN DIEGO, 1899. Early local club members, from left to right, are (front row) Kid Cortez, Jack Keller, and Farrell; (middle row) Sandy Barclay, Jim Little, George Carey, Bert Treanor, and Hugo Klauber; (back row) Elmer Gibbs, Jack Hartley, Tom Works, and Charles VanHorn. (Courtesy San Diego Historical Society, SDHS #94:19293)

FOUR

"Oh, Look Who's Here"

1900–1909

San Diego Population: 17,700
Weather: Sunny, 72 degrees

League officials decided in January of 1900 to allow "northern players" from the California Baseball League to join existing teams, "but to exclude eastern professionals." San Diego filed a protest against Los Angeles for "skimming northerners" before the signing date. It was also agreed "to reserve 2 per cent of the gross receipts of each game for a players' disability fund."

Following the agreement, "northern players" previously with Los Angeles transferred to San Bernardino. The *Union* suspected "a combine among the northern teams who have for their motto. 'Anything to beat San Diego." The Berdoos dropped San Diego into third place with a 6-4 victory on January 21, 1900. It should be noted that at this time, San Diego fielded a team primarily composed of only local talent.

In unrelated news, an eastern visitor created considerable interest when he drove his automobile into San Diego. Using more conventional transportation, 30 cyclists and 200 people in "tally'hos" traveled to El Cajon to follow Commercial League action between Ferris & Ferris and El Cajon. The prominent citizens of El Cajon hosted the game with a gala barbecue of roasted ox and bull heads.

The San Diego town team, back in second place after a 14-1 "drubbing" of league-leading Los Angeles, agreed to face a picked nine from the Commercial League on Washington's Birthday. San Diego won "by one point," 6-5, as the Commercials "did quite well." The only home run in the game was hit over the centerfield fence by 18-year-old Clifford Cravath of the Ferris & Ferris team. A month later, Cravath hit another home run in a Bay View Park game marred by fog, which "made it almost impossible for the fielders to see the batters." Typical of the times, the young slugger had transferred to a new team and, presumably, a better deal.

As the Southern Cal League moved to conclusion, frustration echoed throughout Bay View Park. In the seventh inning of a scoreless game, the fans started to yell: "A dollar for the first run. . . . Two dollars for a home run." The San Diegos responded with nine runs in the final two stanzas to shut out the Seventh Regiment, 9-0. Gibbs and Works collected their money after the game. The Army boys had traveled to San Diego as last minute replacements for the

41

recently folded Athletics team. The next Sunday, the Seventh was replaced by the Pacifics. There was only one week left on the schedule, but the new team promised to be "one of the best in the circuit."

Not surprisingly, the season ended in controversy and confusion. The final standings are unknown. San Diego apparently finished a game or two behind LA and San Bernardino was labeled as "worthy." A professional player named Frank Bowman with experience in the Western and Texas Leagues joined the San Diegos for the season finale against San Bernardino. The "Berdos" were angry because Bowman had played for them the previous Sunday. Apparently the newcomer had stopped to earn a few bucks on his way to San Diego. Fans blamed their team's defeat in San Diego on "the whiskey which the San Bernardino players imbibed the night before the game." The *San Bernardino Sun* accused the players of "the rankest ingratitude" toward the management that had done so much for them.

Another new league was supposed to begin, but rumors persisted that San Diego would not be included because of "the great expense of getting teams there and home again." It was suggested that teams could save $10 to $15 if they traveled with only nine players.

In the meantime, the San Diegos accepted a challenge issued by the Colored Trilbys of Los Angeles to "any nine in Southern California for a purse of $100." The *Union* praised the Trilby club for doing "much to encourage the national game." San Diego won the exciting game in 10 innings, 5-4. Umpire Frank Mertzman was replaced in the fourth inning by CW Averill following a controversial call that went against the Trilbys. The attendance was "rather slim," and the promoters lost $10. One of the organizers, perhaps an attorney, said, "It proves beyond a reasonable doubt that the San Diego public wants league baseball and not exhibition games."

In reality, this was imitation "league baseball" with lesser players. Profits continued to fade through April as gate receipts dropped to $50 a game. Organizers had previously cleared $125 to $175 a game. Profit, the mother's milk of professional sports, helps explain why it would take so long for San Diego to get a team in organized baseball.

Undeterred, another new Southern California Baseball League started in May of 1900, and the San Diego team quickly established itself as the best outfit in the league. There was renewed speculation that Los Angeles would join the California Baseball League in 1901, and San Diego would be included so northern teams could have two stops on their swing into the southland. This was wishful thinking. The Santa Fe Railroad refused to lower fares for baseball teams and the league folded in July.

By August, Jack Dodge was again making efforts to resurrect the Southern California Baseball League for the winter months. He planned to load his team with stars from the "eastern leagues" such as local favorite Sam Dungan, who would lead the American League with a .364 batting average in 1900. A new winter league was confirmed by November. Hope was high (but unrealistic) for a team in the summer California Baseball League. Good ballplayers were expensive and the potential for profit was minimal. It was clear the game, still a sport, was evolving into a business.

Dodge succeeded in importing key members of the Sacramento and Oakland teams. From Sacramento Gilt Edge, the California League champions, San Diego got Charles "Truck" Eagan, William "Brick" Devereaux, and pitcher Charles "Demon" Doyle. Eagan was the Cal League home run leader (11) in 1900 and would lead the Pacific Coast League in home runs for three consecutive years (1903–05). He is a member of the PCL Hall of Fame. Hard-hitting Brick Devereaux was also known as "Wild Bill" for his antics. Charley Doyle was the league's leading pitcher in 1898 and 1899. The Demon was also one of the best batsmen in the league. Hired hands from Oakland included Frank Bowman, Jack Drennan, and Abe Arellanes. The top player was Abe Arellanes who led the California League in batting with a .348 average in 1898. Drennan and Bowman were both solid outfielders for Oakland.

San Diego also obtained the services of "Turkey Mike" Donlin of St. Louis. Donlin was one of the leading hitters of the National League, batting .326 in the recently-completed 1900 season. The *Union* wrote that "he will add that dash and ginger the boys have been in need of."

Turkey would marry popular actress Mabel Hite and compile a lifetime .333 batting average in a 12-year major league career. Rounding out the professionals was a promising young pitcher, Luther "Dummy" Taylor, who would win 114 games over nine years for John McGraw's New York Giants. Special mention is deserved for homegrown San Diego starters, catcher Tom Works and third baseman Hugo Klauber. Works was the son of a former California Supreme Court judge. Klauber's business remains today as the Klauber Wangenheim Company.

Almost 15 inches of rain fell at Campo in February of 1901. The storm damaged Recreation Park and the players helped repair the mess. "The new portion of the grandstand was blown down and 450 feet of the fence on the west side was leveled."

Headlines in the March 4, 1901 *San Diego Union* read, "Broke All Records of Errorless Baseball," "Greatest Game That Was Ever Played in California," "Fifteen Innings Without an Error-San Diego Won." The game received national mention in *The Sporting News* on March 16, 1901: "Almost Perfect. One Run and No Errors Made in 15 Innings. San Diego with the 'Dummy' Pitching Scored a Superb Victory Over San Bernardino." In the past, such hyperbole seemed provincial and naive, but this was a flawless 1-0 game played by respectable professionals.

According to the *Union* article, "There were close to 100 brilliant plays and to pick out a single one would be doing almost an injustice to those who figured in the other ninety-nine." Taylor went the distance for the winners, scattering six hits over 15 innings. Oscar Jones pitched for San Bernardino, surrendering only nine safeties, including the Abe Arellanes single that scored Jack Drennan from second with the game's only run. It was significant that Victor Hugo Klauber was filling in for the injured Mike Donlin at first base. Klauber handled 28 put outs without an error. This was the first time Klauber had ever played this position. Donlin was patrolling right field with a sore arm. *The Sporting News* story made this observation: "One hundred and twenty-seven chances and not a skip . . ."

When the professional players left the following week for their summer jobs, the Southern California Baseball League collapsed from indifference. San Diego was declared the champion with a record of 17 victories, 6 losses, and one tie. This was an outstanding team. There was little coverage of sandlot (amateur) games during the remainder of the year. The term "sandlot" originated in San Francisco during the 1850s when games were played on the site of a former cemetery known as "the Sand Lot." The term was nationally popularized by sportswriters in the Hearst newspaper chain.

In 1908, Clifford "Gavy" Cravath would become San Diego County's first native born major leaguer. For years, official records showed that he played for the 1902 San Diego team in the California League. This was incorrect. San Diego was never in the California League. In a 1914 interview with *The Baseball Magazine*, Cravath stated, "How did I happen to start playing professional baseball? Very simply. The semi-pro team at San Diego needed a catcher, and I needed the money . . . . When I was twenty years old the Los Angeles club signed me for the season." Apparently he was talking about the 1900 San Diego Commercial League. Gavy played third base for Santa Ana when San Diego clubbed the Orange County team, 15-5, in February of 1902.

Interest was keen when Los Angeles came to town for two highly-publicized matches in March of 1902. The first game "looked like a procession." The LA professionals with pitcher Rube Waddell made the locals look like a bunch of rubes. The score was 31-5. The future Hall of Fame hurler went 4 for 6 and smashed the game's only home run.

Colorful and wildly unpredictable, George "Rube" Waddell has been described as "the strangest man to ever play base ball." His nickname could have easily been "Pyro." He once left the mound during a game to chase fire wagons. Teammates had to physically restrain the eccentric from bolting the park at the sound of the fire bell. Rube's severe drinking problem probably contributed to his bizarre behavior. The fans loved him and his buffoonery was good for the box office. Of course, not everything written about Waddell was true . . . but, it has been said, that was only because he had not yet thought to do all the things written about him. Old-time base ball was defined by oddball characters. Rube Waddell was clearly in a league or an orbit of his own.

Because Saturday results were so one-sided, the teams were mixed together for the Sunday game. Rube Waddell thus played with the San Diego nine. Technically speaking, he was the first San Diego player to be enshrined in Cooperstown.

Military baseball was very popular in 1902. Navy battleships would challenge the Army garrison at the San Diego Barracks. In April, veterans Elmer Gibbs and William Kohler were discharged from Battery D "after three years of hard service in China and the [Philippine] islands." During their Far East tour, they played the Marines in the first baseball game in China. Upon entering civilian life, the pair looked to trade their army uniforms for baseball wool in the California League.

Kids played summer baseball at the YMCA camp in Flynn Springs. "Ralph Busnell tried to stop a ball with his nose and had it slightly dislocated." Over 100 rabbits were shot to feed the 18 hungry lads during the two-week encampment.

Chula Vista entered the local baseball scene with surprising success. Sunday games were now commonplace unless you lived in Nebraska City, Nebraska. In July of 1902, the town pastors, known as the Law and Order League, obtained a warrant to stop a ball game scheduled for the Sabbath. Arrests were made. Threats and rocks were hurled in response. Angry farmers rioted and the issue was quickly put to a vote. The good citizens of Nebraska City overwhelmingly decided to play baseball on Sundays.

The West Coast gained a second professional baseball circuit when the Pacific Coast League debuted in 1903. Teams were located in California's four largest cities: Los Angeles, San Francisco, Oakland, and Sacramento. Portland and Seattle were added in the Northwest. The California League folded and was quickly replaced by the new California State League which included smaller communities in the Bay Area. The teams had colorful names like the San Jose Prune Pickers, the Stockton Poppies, the Oakland Haberdashers, and the San Francisco Distillers. Without a clever nickname, how could San Diego stand a chance for consideration from either league? Somehow, "The Bay and Climate Boys" (as they were dubbed in the *Union*) just doesn't compare to the Padres. How do you sew that to a jersey?

The PCL and State League were both "outlaw leagues" that season, outside the jurisdiction of the National Agreement. The Coast League joined Organized Baseball in 1904, but the California State League remained an outlaw for seven years.

Baseball in San Diego was barely mentioned in the *Union* during 1903. On April 11, the Barracks team beat the Normal School, 5-1. The collegians, confident from six victories over La Mesa and Russ High School, learned the soldiers were unbeatable. In June, sailors from the *USS Mohican* battled back to defeat El Cajon, 11-9, in an exciting game. "The Mohican boys put a quietus on the El Cajons' horned and tin-canned applause that was appalling." By the end of summer, in a match between the top service teams, the Navy finally sank the Army, 10-7. Through the efforts and eternal optimism of Jack Dodge, another edition of the Southern California Winter League was formed in December.

San Diego's newest carpetbaggers were primarily the 1902 Oakland Dudes, the same collection that had set a California League record with 108 wins. Prominent among the San Diegos were former Dudes William "Doc" Moskiman, Charles "Buck" Francks, John Walters, Ernest "Kid" Mohler, William "Brick" Devereaux, and Lymon Gorton. Moskiman had posted a 29-22 record for the 1901 Sacramento Senators. Kid Mohler, now 30 years old, was the last of the great left-handed second basemen.

As best can be determined, San Diego finished the campaign with an 8-6 record. Teams were placed in Los Angeles, Santa Barbara, Santa Ana, and San Diego. One of the league stars was Santa Ana's Gavy Cravath. In March, Cravath returned to the PCL Los Angeles Angels. In 1904, talks rekindled to construct another ballpark at the end of the trolley line in University Heights. But instead of "dying quails, ball hawks and goose eggs on the scoreboard," large, awkward birds now strutted their plumage at the end of Park Boulevard. The Coronado Ostrich

Farm had moved across the bay to take up new residence at Mission Cliff Gardens.

A team of "Married Men" defeated "The Single Men" in a "hard fought game." Nob Hill pitcher, Eugene Daney, started for a rare quadruple play against the St. Paul Sunday School team. With the bases loaded, young Daney made a running, jumping catch and threw the ball to second base. It was relayed to "first and then third in time to get all three runners." Middletown School thumped B Street School, 15-4. B Street complained that Middletown used two high school players. In addition to lively San Diego diamond action, baseball was now flourishing in the outlying communities of Fallbrook, Escondido, Oceanside, Vista, Coronado, and El Cajon.

After the Hosp brothers helped Oceanside to victories over San Diego during the Christmas season, the embarrassed Diegos enlisted the services of Albert Carson from Fort Rosecrans. Gunning down 21 Carnation Pickers with his wicked fast ball, the soldier and San Diego tamed the O-Boys, 10-0.

The 1905 Mercantiles were the top club in San Diego County. Logan Heights also boasted a good team known as the East Ends. Sailors, Indians, newspaper boys, high schoolers, fat men, skinny men, and old-timers all enjoyed the national pastime. League ball was limited to local competition. A new ballpark in Coronado was said to be "second to none on the Pacific coast." The Coronado Beach Company donated a 20 1/2-inch "challenge trophy." It was an elegant silver loving cup for the winner of yet another proposed winter league.

In January of 1906, Cycle & Arms beat the Colored Coast Giants, 18-5, on the Middletown Grounds at the foot of Fir Street. The catcher for the "Colored Giants" was William Ritchey, whose son Johnny would become the Jackie Robinson of the Pacific Coast League. In 1948, John Ritchey broke the "color barrier" in the PCL by playing for the San Diego Padres. Other members of the 1906 Giants team included "Fat Sam," Reggie, and Henry. First names were rarely used in base ball articles from that era.

This "colored team" played white teams in a highly competitive commercial league that summer. Something extraordinary happened on June 3, 1906, when the Star Cycle club employed a special battery. "Soldier" Carson of the U.S. Army struck out 23 batters in a 10-inning, 5-4 loss to Cycle & Arms. His catcher was Sanders, a "colored player" with the Coast Giants. It was common practice for the top players to jump from team to team. Regardless of skin color, Sanders was a top player. Almost 100 years ago, there was integration on a San Diego diamond. East End, Star Cycle, and the Coast Giants battled down to the wire. The East Enders eventually took the title with a 5-1 win over Star Cycle on August 19, 1906.

Times were a changin'. Sunday schools across America now recognized baseball as "a moral help," because the game teaches sportsmanship, clean living, manliness, and character. Boys who play Christian baseball on Saturday do not to steal, lie, or cheat.

Another town team formed and beat the best teams from Los Angeles. On November 4, 1906, under the sponsorship of the Pickwick Theater, they defeated Pasadena, 12-2, on the new grounds located at the corner of Twenty-Sixth and Newton Streets.

In December, Southern California Winter League action began. The Pickwicks were off to a disappointing start in league action when they faced Hal Chase's American League team on New Year's Day 1907. Although the big leaguers had beaten San Diego, 14-8, the Pickwick team was coming together and starting to win games. Franz Hosp pitched 31 innings of scoreless ball. The leading batters were Jack Hartley (.430), followed by James Colbarth (.387), and John "Chief" Meyers (.379) who would play nine years in the National League. The popular Riverside Indian became a member of McGraw's Giants and is best remembered as the Christy Mathewson's catcher.

San Diego had climbed to third place in February when they met a team from Anaheim that was described as "a bunch of farmers." The ragtag visitors wore three different types of uniforms, but they had an impressive kid on the mound. The Anaheim boys "say he belongs in their neck of the woods and that he is not a ringer in any sense of the word." Walter Johnson and his

Farmers won, 2–1.

The following weekend, the rowdy Los Angeles Morans were unable to make rail connections, so the Pickwicks played the USS Boston instead. The Jacktars put up a good fight before losing, 4-2. San Diego would go on to win most of the remaining games on their schedule. League standings were not published during the season, which was usually an indication that the San Diegos did not win the championship.

The Pickwicks invited the mighty Los Angeles Angels to Athletic Field for an exhibition game in March. Although fans kicked about the high ticket prices (fifty cents), the increase was necessary to entice the PCL team down to San Diego. Pitcher Franz Hosp, the pride of Oceanside, was brilliant in a losing cause. The Angels were lucky to squeak out a 1-0 victory. LA manager Henry Berry was emphatic: "San Diego has by far the best amateur team in the state." Hosp signed with the Angels and "San Diego loses one of the best players that has ever trod a local diamond."

Another league formed in April and the standings were printed now because the Pickwicks quickly grabbed first place. This was a tough circuit with competitive teams from Los Angeles, San Bernardino, and Pasadena. The colorful Hoegee Flags were favorites with future big league star Fred Snodgrass on their roster. The team, sponsored by an LA sporting goods store, wore flags from different nations on the back of their uniforms. They would battle the Pickwicks to the very end. On June 30, the Hoegees took first place from the Pickwicks with a 9-3 victory. After the game, the large crowd remained to watch Professor Richard Ericson make a balloon ascension. They gasped when the daring Ericson leaped out of the balloon. Fortunately, the professor had packed a parachute. He floated safely to earth.

In September, San Diego would pop the Hoegee's balloon with a three game sweep to claim the league flag. Manager Will Palmer again brazenly issued another challenge to Los Angeles. The Angels had just won the Pacific Coast League championship with an impressive record of 115 wins and 74 losses.

Eventually the Angels, erstwhile the Loo Loos, agreed to terms for a five-game series to be held in San Diego. The prize was Palmer's mythical Pacific Coast Championship of 1907. The bush Pickwicks had a ringer in the box.—Walter Johnson. On November 7, 1907, the Big Train struck out 16 Angels as the Pickwicks took the opener, 1-0. Johnson even drove in the game's only run with a long sacrifice fly in the seventh inning. Pickwick captain Chief Meyers collected three hits including a double.

Southpaw "Dolly" Gray won 32 games for the Angels in 1907. The Pickwicks would counter in the second game with local favorite Albert "Soldier" Carson. The hometown *Union* was certain Carson would win, but Gray and the Loo Loos prevailed, 5-2. Meyers took one of Carson's "outshoots" on his finger tip and had to be scratched for the remainder of the series.

Game three would last 12 innings with Los Angeles scoring four times in the top of the twelveth for an 8-4 victory. San Diego was furious about several questionable calls made by the umpire. The angry arbiter stalked off the field in the ninth inning and had to be replaced. The *Union* reported, "There is not the slightest doubt but that Karns is one of the most unpopular umpires who ever handled an indicator on a San Diego diamond."

Los Angeles led the series two games to one, and a doubleheader was scheduled the following morning to play the deciding game or games as the case may be. This is when things got weird— real weird. The same Jack Karns who had the umpired the first three games would pitch the early game for the Pickwicks. The outcome of this melodrama would hinge on a match-up between Franzel Hosp, a popular former hurler for the Pickwicks, and a new San Diego spitballer who had just been unmercifully berated by the fans and his own teammates.

Initially Hosp was in command for the Angels. Los Angeles clung to a 1-0 lead when somehow San Diego scored four times in the fifth inning without benefit of a hit. The last run crossed the plate while the Loo Loos were arguing a call. The new umpire was Ralph Frary, an experienced professional from the Northwest League. During the beef, LA shortstop Walter

"Judge" Nagle made a serious error in judgment. He referred to Umpire Frary with an uncomplimentary name. The humorless arbitrator "promptly put his good right fist to the aforesaid 'judge's' jaw and the latter lost no time in reaching his playing position."

With one out in the sixth inning, the visitors pulled to within one run. The bags were full of Angels when Karns was forced to leave the game with an injured hand. Enter Walter Johnson, held in reserve if needed to pitch the afternoon game on two days rest. The Big Train induced an inning-ending double play, then held Los Angeles scoreless over the final three stanzas to preserve a 4-3 Pickwicks victory.

At 3:30 p.m., the indomitable Johnson returned to the mound to start the championship game. His opponent, Dolly Gray, winner of game two, would work on one day's rest. Los Angeles had no intentions of losing this so-called championship to a bunch of bushers from San Diego. Both pitchers were lit up, but the Angels hit Johnson harder and prevailed, 9-3. The big right-hander had developed a sore arm and reportedly lobbed the ball after the third inning. In the end, Will Palmer and his Pickwicks had made their point. Johnson recovered from the ordeal to win 411 more games over the next 20 years as a Washington Senator. The great right-hander was one of five original Hall of Fame inductees at Cooperstown in 1936.

Another winter league immediately hatched. The plan was to have the Angels and a team of "Eastern League" (major league) all-stars join this "fast" circuit. Fans were sternly admonished that if they did not support "classy ball in San Diego, the 10-cent corner lot variety will again be dominant." "Classy ball" was defined as the 50-cent variety. Attendance figures were poor. The classy league had to down-size to a two team "series." The final results: LA Ralstons five wins, Pickwicks four wins and one tie.

Undaunted or simply blind to reality, the Pickwicks next looked to join the outlaw California State League for the summer of 1908. The organizers pointed out the team's success in the recent Pacific Coast Championships, but forgot they could no longer rent Walter Johnson. Regardless, on March 8, 1908, San Diego ambushed the Oakland Oaks, 15-2. The next day, the Chicago White Sox did an encore on the same PCL team, 13-6. The Pickwicks may have been for real, but would San Diego cranks shell out four bits to support them in a real league?

Instead of joining the faster Cal State League, the Pickwicks began the summer in an ill-defined Southern State League. After a few games, they decided to wait until winter for the pursuit of glory and, more importantly, increased gate receipts. The 1908–09 Pickwicks turned out to be even better than advertised. It appears their final record was 17-2. On February 28, 1909, manager Will Palmer, his buttons popping with pride, accepted the "blue silk pennant heavily trimmed with gold braid and lace, the lettering being of white silk and as follows, 'Championship, California Winter League, Won by San Diego.'"

Baseball had become popular recreation on the reservation in 1909. The Pala Warriors held their own against strong town teams in the North San Diego County. The Indians had a fine battery which consisted of Albert Gulch and Blacktooth.

Billed as "The Night Championship of the West," the PCL's San Francisco Seals and Los Angeles Angels would meet under electric lights at Chutes Park in LA on October 9, 1909. Sufficient lighting apparatus would be on hand to make "the park brighter than day." 4,000 fans attended the exhibition won by the Angels, 17-11. "Scores of arc lights were used and several theater spotlights were employed to follow the course of the ball and the base runners. One of the poles was stationed in the center of the diamond just back of the pitcher." For the sake of safety, pitches were thrown underhand which resulted in an "old fashioned score." The nine-inning game lasted less than an hour because the players were swinging on the first pitch. When Turkey Mike Donlin heard the idea, he moaned, "You can't take a player's nights away from him."

The decade ended with San Diego at 8-3, a game behind first-place Santa Barbara (9-2) in the Winter League. During the Christmas game with Pasadena, the temperature was so high that rooters "even took off their coats to lessen the warmth." This was a time when gentlemen wore a coat and tie to the ball game. League balance improved when Walter Johnson joined Santa Ana. As the Celery Raisers began to climb in the standings, transportation problems threatened to destroy the entire circuit.

RUSS HIGH SCHOOL BASE BALL TEAM, 1900. San Diego High School was still known as Russ High in 1900. Their base ball team won one game that year . . . the last game of the season when they defeated the local Commercial College, 8-3. (Courtesy San Diego Historical Society, SDHS OP #15567)

FOURTH OF JULY, 1900. Holiday base ball became an American institution in the 1800s. During that same time, because of our favorable climate, more games were played in San Diego on Thanksgiving and Christmas. With the turn of the new century, the Fourth of July ball game became as important to the local celebration as brass bands and fireworks. Game day participants, seen above from left to right, are (standing) Henry Myers, Rufus Choate, AH Biewener, (Uncle Sam) Colonel Ed Fletcher, CF VanHorn, Gene Williams, and Tom Works; (seated) Claude Woolman and Alex Reynolds. (Courtesy San Diego Historical Society, SDHS #94:19291)

ELKS BASE BALL TEAM. In an amateur game played at Bay View Park on July 14, 1900, the Elks from Lodge 168 trampled the Wheelmen, 22-1. (Courtesy San Diego Historical Society, SDHS #14693)

left: **GROUP AT SAN DIEGO, 1900.** Early base ball promoter Jack Dodge rounded up this "group" of fun-loving professionals for the 1900–01 winter season. Pictured, from left to right, are (seated) "Turkey" Mike Donlin and Jack Drennan. Back; (standing) Charles "Truck" Eagan, Abe Arellanes, and Bill "Brick" Devereaux. Fred Lange, a contemporary, described his friends as follows: "Truck Eagan, a great ballplayer, a wonderful hitter and a fine fellow to meet and play with. Truck could hit them as far as anybody I have known. Abe [Arellanes] was one of that family of good ball players from Santa Cruz. Abe was a fast fielder, base runner and a good hitter, not a weakness. Bill [Devereaux] to my notion was one of the most congenial and best-liked ball players on the Pacific Coast, full of fun, but not neglecting his duties as a player. Lower right is a prince of a fellow, Jack Drennan, a wonderful fielder, hitter and good all-round player, a gentleman on and off the diamond, one of the best-looking players on the Coast."

right: **MIKE DONLIN AND MABEL HITE.** Fred Lange continued: "Below, on the left [of the group picture], is the great Mike Donlin. He was good at any position and a very fine hitter and base runner, he could also throw. He was twelve years in the National League and hit better than .300 each year [actually better than .300 in ten of his twelve years]. A clever, hard-working player at all times. In 1905 Mike's hitting and Christy Mathewson's pitching won the championship for their team, also the World Series from the Philadelphia Athletics. Mike also was the captain of the New York team from 1906–10. He discontinued baseball to go on the vaudeville stage as an actor and married Mabel Hite, an actress. Mike and his wife made a very fine-looking couple, as you can see from this photograph. They were quite successful on the stage, but Mike returned to baseball in 1914 with the Boston Braves (after his wife died of cancer at age 27) and was sold to Pittsburgh, where he finished his baseball career in 1916 . . . a hale fellow well met."

SOUVENIR OF 1901 TEAM. "A group picture of the San Diego team was taken a few days ago. It will make an interesting souvenir after the team disbands and many of the players leave." (*San Diego Union*, February 13, 1901.) Buy yours now at the San Diego Historical Society. (Courtesy San Diego Historical Society, SDHS #23486)

BROKE ALL RECORDS
OF ERRORLESS BASEBALL.

GREATEST GAME THAT WAS EVER PLAYED IN CALIFORNIA.

Fifteen Innings Without an Error—San Diego Won
—Levys Lost Again in Los Angeles—
Gossip of the Game.

The San Diego and San Bernardino baseball teams gave the cranks of San Diego something to talk about for years to come, by playing what was in many respects the most remarkable baseball game ever played in the state of California. The San Bernardino left if the sixth man had not made the circuit, and won the game. Of the 46 put-outs, twenty-one on each side were made at first base, eight on one side and seven on the other went out on flies to the field, and there was not a ball hit into the air which could be reached that was not pulled down by someone.

L.H. TAYLOR

Luther M. Taylor, one of the pitchers of the New York Club, was born s s Feb. 21, 1876, at Olathe, Kas., and learned to play ball whe a a student in the deaf and dumb institute in that city. In 1895 he made his debut as a professional wi.. the Shreveport Club of the Southern League. After the disbandment of that organization on June 1, he joined the Mattoon team of the Central League. He started the season of 1896 with the Albany team of the New York State League and remained with it until late in August, when the New York Club purchased his release. Last winter he pitched for the San Diego team of the Southern California League. The Cleveland American League Club negotiated with him and claimed to have signed him for this season, but the New York Club secured him at a hand-some increase in salary over what he received in 1900. Taylor shows great improvement in his work of late and Manager Davis considers him one of his best pitchers.

HEADLINES FROM *SAN DIEGO UNION*, MARCH 2, 1901, AND LUTHER "DUMMY" TAYLOR.

Up, Up, and Away. The 1902 Los Angeles team is shown in a hot air balloon. Seated near the middle (holding a dog) with LA on his jersey is pitcher Rube Waddell, "the strangest man to ever play base ball." Los Angeles beat San Diego so thoroughly that Waddell switched teams for the second game of the series. Technically, this qualifies Rube as the first San Diego player to be inducted into the Baseball Hall of Fame. (Courtesy Mark Macrae)

1903 SAN DIEGO NORMAL SCHOOL TEAM. This is the first known picture of a San Diego State baseball team. Their first recorded game was played in 1899 and they lost to La Mesa, 36-3. By 1903, the Normals could handle Russ High School and La Mesa, but the soldiers at the Army Barracks proved too tough for the college boys.

1904 SAN DIEGO SCHOOL. The core of San Diego's 1903–04 Winter League team were members of the Oakland Dudes, champions of the 1902 California League. Team members, from left to right, are (front row) George Hodson, Walter "Judge" McCredie, and Henry Schmidt; (back row) John Walters, Lymon Gorton, Charles "Buck" Francks, Ernest "Kid" Mohler, "Brick" Devereaux, Julius "Jules" Streib, Bill Dunleavy, Billy Cristall, and manager Pete Lohman. Kid Mohler was the last of the great left-handed second basemen. He was later the baseball coach for the US Naval Academy at Annapolis.

Cycle and Arms	ab.	r.	bh.	po.	a.	e.
B. Harris, c	5	1	0	9	1	1
Miller, 1b	5	1	1	14	0	0
Lambert, lf	2	0	1	0	0	0
Wilson, lf	3	1	1	0	0	0
Hosp, p	3	1	0	2	2	1
Campbell, 2b	3	1	1	1	3	2
Hayawrd, ss	4	0	0	0	2	1
Hesser, rf	5	0	1	0	0	1
Shaw, cf	4	0	0	2	0	0
D. Harris, 3b	4	0	0	2	5	2
Totals..............	38	5	5	30	13	8

Star Cycles	ab.	r.	bh.	po.	a.	e.
Poole, cf	5	0	1	0	0	0
Lopey, 1b	5	0	0	5	0	1
Surano, 2b	4	1	0	0	1	0
Eggling, 3b	4	2	2	1	0	1
Starr, ss	4	0	2	0	0	1
Mundell, lf	4	0	1	0	0	1
Carson, p	4	0	0	1	2	0
Reinert, rf	4	0	0	1	0	0
Sanders, c	3	1	0	22	3	0
Totals..............	37	4	6	30	6	4

Sanders of the Coast Giants caught for the Star Cycles and Carson for the army team was in the box. Carson struck out twenty-three men of the thirty put out, and if he had support equal to his pitching there would have been a different ending to the game.

ZEENUT SERIES PC LEAGUE CARSON VERNON

JOHNNY RITCHEY, BOX SCORE, AND AL "SOLDIER" CARSON. In 1948, Johnny Ritchey (left) broke the "color barrier" for the Pacific Coast League when he played with his hometown Padres. In 1906, his father, William Ritchey, starred for one of San Diego's earliest "colored teams"—the Coast Giants—a team that primarily played against white competition. On June 3, 1906, one of Ritchey's Coast Giants teammates, a catcher named Sanders, became the first black ballplayer to play on an integrated team in San Diego. He was the battery mate of future Chicago Cubs pitcher Al "Soldier" Carson (right), on the Star Cycles team.

BASEBALL GAME AT POWAY COMMUNITY CHURCH. Baseball was now encouraged by Sunday schools, because the game taught sportsmanship, clean living, manliness, and character. Boys who play Christian baseball on Saturday do not to steal, lie, or cheat. (Courtesy San Diego Historical Society, SDHS #16355)

LOGAN HEIGHTS SCHOOL BASEBALL TEAM, 1907. (Courtesy San Diego Historical Society, SDHS #12414)

W.H. OTTO BASEBALL TEAM, 1909. We know there was a Logan Heights School, but W.H.O. was W.H. Otto? Mr. Otto sponsored a good looking young ball team with fine looking uniforms, but who was H.E? (Courtesy San Diego Historical Society, SDHS #OP-15163-3)

SAN DIEGO PICKWICKS AT BAY VIEW PARK, 1907. Pictured above, from left to right, are Walter "The Big Train" Johnson, Jack Karns, Chief Meyers, Jack Clynes, Al Carson, Will Palmer, Fred Bergeman, Jack Hartley, Langdon, Hunky Shaw, Joe McCarty, Tom Downey, and WT Hanrahan. This important photograph is a good example of how players can get

PICKWICK THEATRE TEAM, CARTOON, AND PROGRAM. Baseball promoter Will Palmer owned the Pickwick Theatre, so it was only natural he would name his team the San Diego Pickwicks. *Left:* His players, from left to right, are (front row) Charles VanHorn, Early Starr, WT Hanrahan, Bert Treanor, and Orlando Cole; (middle row) Jack Karns, Jim Colbath, Jack Hartley, and Joe Cauthorne; (back row) Tom Works, the Palmer Brothers—Oscar, Will, Edgar, and Scott—and Joe McCarty. (Courtesy San Diego Historical Society, SDHS #14673) *Right:* The Pickwick Theatre program contained advertisements for the series with the Los Angeles Angels and assorted base ball supplies. The cartoon appeared after San Diego won the first game.

misidentified. Over the years, this picture has been published several times with some of the players listed as Franz Hosp, Jack Killelay, Hugh Kallackey, Chick Autry, and Pug Bennett. Hosp, an Oceanside native, often played for San Diego teams. However, in this series, he was with the Los Angeles Angels. (Courtesy San Diego Historical Society, SDHS #11931 detail)

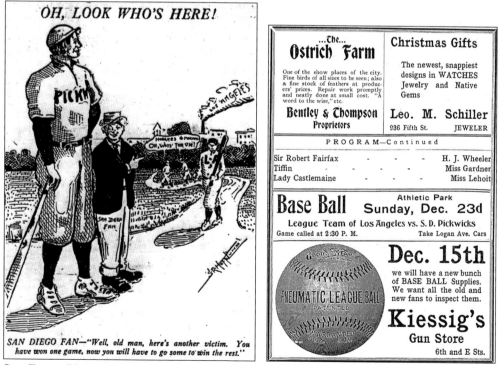

SAN DIEGO UNION, NOVEMBER 8, 1907. (Courtesy SDHS Ephemera Collection)

SALT LAKE BASE BALL TEAM. Salt Lake had one of the better teams in the California Winter League from 1908 through 1910. California had begun to draw eastern clubs during the winter months. (Courtesy San Diego Historical Society, SDHS #2987)

SAN DIEGO BASE BALL TEAM, 1909–1910. In the middle row are "Cannibal Joe" McCarty, Chief Meyers, and Franzell Hosp. Others in photo may include Almgren and Luis Estudillo. (Courtesy San Diego Historical Society, SDHS #3627-1)

FIVE

"A Real Ball Team. . ."

1910–1919

San Diego Population: 39,578
Weather: Sunny, 72 degrees

Serious trouble was brewing in the 1910 Southern California Winter League. Home teams could avoid payment of visitor transportation costs by the unilateral cancellation of games at the slightest hint of inclement weather. Everybody knows it never rains in Southern California, but Santa Ana prematurely canceled a game with San Diego at the "threat of wet grounds." In an unrelated fair-weather issue, Santa Barbara refused to advance full fare tickets, so manager Will Palmer paid for the Barbarians to take the train down to Athletic Park. The league leaders were thumped, 7-1, and San Diego moved into a first-place tie with the Channel City team.

Thoroughly frustrated, the San Diegos dropped out of the league the next weekend when Santa Ana refused to play in a drizzle. According to the *Union*, ". . . the diamond was hard and firm," but "Manager Crolic of the celery raisers was obdurate and called his hands off. They took the afternoon train for the north." Obviously, Palmer had made the mistake of prepaying the round trip tickets for the visitors.

San Diego went independent and captured a 10-inning, 1-0 win from Annis "the white slabster" (pitcher) and his Colored LA Occidental teammates. San Diego's captain, 'Pug' Bennett was "conspicuous by his absence." A foot injury was claimed "but it is said that the real reason was a disinclination to play against a negro team." A total of four games, all won by San Diego, were played with the Occidentals. The final contest "threatened to develop into a genuine race riot" with hard feelings on both sides.

A crack Japanese team from Los Angeles, described as "little brown men," was scheduled to face San Diego on February 20, 1910. "The weather prophets at Los Angeles foretold rain." The *Union* headline scolded, "Jap Aggregation Fails to Appear." The next weekend, San Diego defeated Chicago White Sox pitcher "Death Valley" Jim Scott (who would twice become a 20-game winner in the American League) and a team of Japanese position players, 1-0, in a game shortened by transportation problems. Manager Palmer decided to "wait til next year."

A Field Day for San Diego grammar school children was held on May 14, at Athletic Field.

Since grass had not yet been invented, a sprinkling cart was used to keep the dust down. Lincoln narrowly defeated Sherman for the overall championship. The other schools (in order of finish) included Logan, Florence, Middletown, Franklin, and University Heights.

A local summer league formed with teams from the Gas Company, the Soldiers (Fort Rosecrans), Cycle & Arms, and Russ Lumber. The season opened with "a monster automobile parade" to Athletic Park. In non-league action, the San Diego Police lost to the Firemen, 28-8, with this headline: "Was'nt (sic) It Awful, Mabel?" After another game between the flat feet and the press, this insult appeared in the caption above the pictures: "Policemen Play Ball Like 'Aunt Ruth,' Championship Aggregation of Scribes Defeats Fat Coppers; Score 10-9."

With a 47-13 record, Albert G. Spalding pitched the Chicago White Stockings (Cubs) to the first National League pennant in 1876. This baseball pioneer, sporting goods tycoon, and future Hall of Famer later retired to Point Loma where his wife served as one of Madame Tingley's leading disciples in her mysterious Church of Theosophy. Efforts were made in 1910 to entice Spalding to run on the Republican ticket for the United States Senate. In those days, Republican candidates were almost assured election in California. One of Spalding's campaign promises was to host the 1915 World Series in San Francisco. According to the *San Diego Union*, Spalding was seemingly his party's choice, but the nomination instead went to the Honorable Thomas J. Works. The former state Supreme Court justice and father of early San Diego ballist, Tom Works, won the trip to Washington.

A four-team winter league that included the "colored" Chicago Leland Giants began in November of 1910. The San Diego Bears were barely over .500 (7-6) when professionals Gavy Cravath and Carl Lewis joined the team. Cravath hit a home run on January 2, 1911, and the Bears nipped the McCormicks, 3-2, to move into a first-place tie with the Los Angeles club. San Diego would go on to reel off 16 straight victories and coast to the Southern California championship.

At the end of the season, the Leland Giants came to town for a meaningless series. Gambling was heavy that San Diego would win the final game. Then word spread quickly through the stands that "all bets on this game have been declared off." Although several Giants were allegedly in on the fix, the Lelands took both ends of the twin bill.

In May of 1911, because of civil unrest in Mexico, the Army conducted maneuvers along the international border. On Sundays, the soldiers relaxed and presented drills, lectures, band concerts, and baseball games for the public to enjoy. By this time, Navy teams were always looking for competition with local clubs.

Shields Transfer, with veterans like Jack Hartley, Tom Works, and Charles Van Horn, was the class team of the summer County Baseball League. Promotions included weekly giveaways for the players: shoes, hats, and theater box seat tickets offered by local merchants for home runs. One week, four players enjoyed fine stage productions at the Empress Theater.

Bizarre baseball was courageously reported when Blind Bill Darrow spun a no-hitter for the *Union-Tribune* against the *San Diego Sun*. The final score was 22-19. In the contest, described as "weird and grotesque," Darrow successfully found home plate often enough to strike out 15 Suns. More often than not, he was unable to locate the dish and walked perhaps three times as many . . . when he wasn't hitting them with fast balls.

A new winter league for local teams lasted for only a month and was pronounced dead by the San Diego *Union* on December 11. The observation was made that San Diego bugs (fans) only "support good baseball." The "fans favor the one team plan, the club to be managed by some person who has had experience." The popular sentiment was to see San Diego united against outside teams; however, a professional league failed to materialize in the winter of 1911–12.

Newspaper accounts covered sandlot, service, grammar and high school baseball games. Descendants of San Diego's earliest settlers and original ballists now formed one of the city's better teams. Tony Serrano's Old Town Mexicans were beating everybody in 1912.

A picked nine of former San Diego high schoolers and winter leaguers met the Santa Fe Red Cap Porters at Athletic Field on the Fourth of July. The black porters prevailed, 1-0. It was said,

"An adverse decision at the plate entered largely in the shutout for the San Diegans." The Red Caps, strictly a road team, knew that local umpires can be rough.

The top game of the summer was negotiated between National City and San Diego. Wagering grew and San Diego began adding ringers, but National City had a secret weapon. "Soldier" Riddle whitewashed the big city boys, 1-0. The next time they met, San Diego reloaded and clubbed their southern neighbors, 14-7.

The San Diego Theatrical Baseball League formed in September. Teams included the Spreckels, Pantages, Empress, and Savoy Theaters. Results of these games are sketchy at best. This much is known: ". . . everybody became inoculated with the bingling insect's bite and went after the leather in 'Texas Tommy' style, plunking the daylights out of it, losing six spheres and tearing the cover off three or four more." Imagine the pathos, the drama, the comedy of San Diego's legitimate theater employees taking on the rabble moving picture workers. Next time you visit the neighborhood multiplex, think about the staff playing "Texas Tommy" baseball. Incidentally, the Savoy Faires claimed the 1912 Theatrical League Championship.

Real baseball returned in November. The Bears had clawed their way to first place with a 7-3 record when both Tufts-Lyon and the McCormicks "pulled up stakes as far as playing any more games of the winter league schedule at Los Angeles." Officially, their decision was blamed on poor attendance. Realistically, these teams just could not match up with either San Diego or Rube Foster's Chicago American Giants.

Rube Foster would become the Father of the Negro Leagues. Historian John Holway wrote, "White baseball had never seen anyone quite like Rube Foster. He was Christy Mathewson, John McGraw, Connie Mack, Al Spalding, and Kenesaw Mountain Landis—great pitcher, manager, owner, league organizer, czar—all rolled into one." The American Giants evolved from the Leland Giants. Prior to the Winter League fold, the Bears had mauled the Giants in four of their six games. Up to this point, cartoons and coverage in the *Union* can only be described as elitist and racist. Then something very interesting happened. San Diego's only equal on the diamond was the colored team. If they wanted to play and fill the stands with paying customers, they had to reconcile themselves to play a black team . . . all of the time.

During the winter of 1912–1913, the Bears and Giants would meet a total of 24 times. San Diego won 14 and Chicago took 10 games. The hard feelings that marred the early games had slowly changed into mutual respect between the players, black and white. There was also a change of attitude in *Union* reports: "The American Giants are the only players in southern California that have really caused the locals to extend themselves to their limit, and caused any doubt as to who's who and why."

Fans had thought the Bears 1910–11 championship season was the pinnacle. This Bears team was even better. San Diego fans had never witnessed such a level of sustained excellence. The following excerpt is from a March 23, 1913 article in the *Union*:

> *In after years those of us who will hold berths in the 'inside' circuit can turn pages back through dusty memories and tell the newcomers to San Diego that once upon a time San Diego had a real ball team. And right here it should be written that these aforesaid Giants played ball of high caliber of quality that could be compared with the work of major league teams. Every time the Bears and Giants met at Athletic Park it was a battle. Every run and every play was of importance.*

Before the start of the Coast League season, the Portland Beavers scheduled a five-game series with the American Giants. Rube Foster's team won four of those five games. "McCredie [Beavers manager Walter "Judge" McCreedie] concedes that several of the dusky men are of major league caliber and that only the drawing of the color line forces them out of organized baseball." How good was Portland? That year the Beavers would go on to win the Pacific Coast League championship.

Nineteen Thirteen was a watershed year for baseball in San Diego. The Southern California

Class D League formed and San Diego got one of the teams. The owner was former major league veteran Duff "Dick" Cooley, who had received early retirement in 1906 when he was replaced in the Detroit outfield by a flash named Ty Cobb. Subsequently, Cooley had experience operating successful minor league teams in Topeka and Salt Lake City. He sold his interest in the Salt Lake club to partner Bill "Hardrock" Lane in 1912 and used the money to purchase the San Diego franchise.

On April 22, 1913, a grand Opening Day automobile parade was delayed temporarily because Mr. Cooley had failed to obtain the proper permits. An hour late at Athletic Park, the ceremonial first pitch was more-or-less tossed by Mayor-elect Charles F. O'Neall. The totally new and mighty San Diego Bears took the field in their navy blue uniforms. They dropped a heartbreaker to the Pasadena Millionaires, 4-2. Regardless, the fans were "thrilled by snappy ball" and the confident Cooley assured the multitude, "We will get after them strong tomorrow."

Dick Cooley was absolutely correct. San Diego won the next day, the next day after that, and day after day following. A week later, the Bears were pulling away from the league with a 9-1 record. An unexpected problem occurred when Pasadena ministers strongly protested playing baseball on the Sabbath. The equally pious clergy of Long Beach, "which has the most drastic anti-liquor ordinance in the state," also vehemently opposed Sunday baseball. Major scheduling changes were made to avoid further hell and brimstone from the pulpit.

By the end of May, the 29-8 Bears were lapping the field. The "pure cities," Pasadena and Long Beach, were struggling along at 11-26 and 12-25, respectively. Attendance was dwindling throughout the circuit. Bears manager Spencer Abbott was sent to Pasadena in an effort to save a team that would eventually seek redemption in Santa Barbara.

Cooley sold brilliant young shortstop Charles Flanagan to the St. Louis Browns for the princely sum of $3,500. Sailor Flanagan had only been able to play home games pending his discharge from the Navy on June 27. Two days later, the ingrate demanded $500 of the sale price. Cooley refused to consider this outrageous request. Charlie Flanagan learned quickly that it was as difficult to hit a major league curve ball as it was to separate "a handful of C notes" from a base ball owner. The surly sailor disappeared into obscurity after three hitless plate appearances for the lowly 1913 American Leaguers. The Brownies would finish in last place and their catcher, Sam Agnew, would lead the league with 28 errors. Remember that name: Sam Agnew.

The outlook was bright for San Diego in the Southern California League standings. The Bears had captured the first half of the season with a 46-24 mark. Talent had been redistributed through the league to help achieve balance, but it was disturbing to learn that the Long Beach and Santa Barbara players were not being paid. On July 14, the Barbarians packed their bags for a third home in Bakersfield. They never made it. The Long Beach Beachcombers were already broke.

Dick Cooley proclaimed, "The league is dead." Somehow his fellow owners expected a share of the money he received from the Flanagan deal. Of course, they got nothing. Baseball is not communism. Cooley complained bitterly about San Diego: "I can't understand the people, and I don't believe they'll make baseball pay here in a thousand years. I'm convinced they don't want baseball in San Diego."

The *Union* groaned in harmony: "A detail of police would be necessary to get a dozen fans to another game." Somehow a two-team league survived until the end of July when the Bears drowned the San Bernardino Kittens in an uninspired death match. In retrospect, Dick Cooley had created a team that was too good for Class D competition and San Diego bugs were spoiled by the high caliber of play they enjoyed in the winter leagues. Professional baseball in San Diego would become forgotten history.

Parades are always popular. Before the year was out, there would be another big one through town. Racecar driver Olin Davis, champion of the San Diego Exposition Race with his powerful Locomobile, "the San Diego boys, winners of the greatest motorcycle race in history—the mad dash from here to Phoenix," and hundreds of other fancy automobiles would participate in this gala motorized salute to champions from the world of sport. Also honored were Southwest clay pigeon marksman Andrew J. Ervast, the San Diego Rowing Club (winners of the California barge championship), the Chicago White Sox, and the New York Giants. Wait a minute. Why would San Diego honor the Sox and Giants?

Charles Comiskey and John McGraw decided to visit San Diego to play an exhibition as part of their world wide crusade to spread baseball to Asia, Africa, Europe, and back across the Atlantic. It was made clear that the purpose of the trip "is not for profit." Game ticket prices ranged from "a dollar or four bits" and "exactly 4,386 persons separated themselves from a stack of legal tender" even though the great Christy Mathewson would not pitch in San Diego.

By all accounts, they were not disappointed; not until the game was called suddenly by darkness with the score tied 3-3 in the ninth inning. The angry crowd poured onto the field to register protest. Umpire Bill Klem wisely ruled that play should resume. Jim Scott grooved his first pitch to Chief Meyers and the Giants catcher took a healthy swing. "Scott glanced up, saw the sphere disappear in the region of the bay, and walked off the field." Meyers, the former Pickwick favorite, "was swallowed up in the mob that swarmed over the diamond as he touched the bases and his name was shouted from the throats of thousands."

An eight-team Winter Association began play in November. Since most of the Los Angeles teams were without home fields, all of the Bears' games were scheduled for Athletic Park. Chief Meyers, back in town for the off-season, used his "war club" to beat Mathies of Los Angeles into submission, and San Diego began a run of nine consecutive victories. Manager Will Palmer found a new sponsor and the Bears became the Quality Brewers. Palmer added a pair of outstanding pitchers who had just returned from their worldwide tour: Reb Russell of the White Sox and Jeff Tesreau of the Giants. On January 4, 1914, the Qualities finally lost to Charlie Chech and Hap Hogan's San Bernardino Stars. Palmer took his team north on February 15, and Tesreau whitewashed the San Berdoos. The Giants right-hander would go on to lead the National League with eight shutouts in 1914.

It was reported in the *Union* that Comiskey and McGraw, who had professed no interest in turning a profit, made $75,000 off their baseball odyssey. Apparently transportation, player salaries, and room and board only cost $25,000. The players had to be scratching their heads. Comiskey was a notorious skinflint, a trait that would lead to great scandal in the World Series six years later.

The "biggest game of 1914" was contested on February 28, between the Lambs and Goats of the Cuyamaca Club at Athletic Park. Banks closed at noon. "Beautiful women and bright girls" were among the 3,000 enthusiastic fans who cheered and giggled as the single guys (Lambs) pounded out a convincing 13-9 victory over their married counterparts (Goats). Society folk were pleased with the extensive attention and coverage afforded their ladies, gents, pets, humor, and unique lifestyles.

Later that summer in Commercial League action, Savage Tire ran over Western Metal Supply Company. When the Padres came to town, Western Metal Supply became the exclusive distributor for official Pacific Coast League baseballs. Winter League baseball would be a local affair in 1914–1915. The Marine Corps started strong, but the Wanderers eventually claimed the city championship from Spreckels Theater. The Wanderers, mostly former San Diego High School ballplayers reunited by their old coach, Pug Bennett, were given gold watch fobs. On the last day of the season, the Marines dropped Cycle & Arms into the cellar before an enthusiastic crowd at makeshift Exposition Park in Balboa Park.

A barnstorming troupe of National and American League stars played in San Diego during the winter of 1915. The Nationals, with Grover Cleveland Alexander drawing mound duty for the third consecutive day in the third different city, shut out the American League, 1-0. Art Fletcher manufactured the game's only run with bold base running in the ninth inning. "Bullet Joe" Bush of Connie Mack's AL Champs took the loss. Rain was blamed for the small turnout as only 1,500 hearty souls braved the elements to watch big league baseball. Rain has always sent San Diego indoors.

In March 1915, Will Palmer arranged a series of games between the Indianapolis Indians of the American Association and Hap Hogan's Venice Tigers in San Diego. In the first game, the Hoosiers took a one-run lead into the ninth, but the Coast Leaguers rallied for an 8-7 victory. The following day, Venice again beat Indianapolis and then knocked off the powerful Chicago White Sox on the third afternoon. Even with Eddie Collins, "America's Greatest Ball Player," none of the three games drew more than 1,000 spectators.

Magnificent City Stadium (renamed Balboa Stadium in 1939) on the campus of San Diego High School, hailed as "the greatest public playground in the United States," opened with a display of great civic pride on May 31, 1915. Although primarily designed for football and track, a diamond with a grass infield and a short left field porch was also part of the layout. With this new venue, several amateur leagues emerged, including the San Diego Bank League complete with banker's hours.

For the first time in years, San Diego had a summer semi-pro team known as the Bee Gees. They were hard-nosed ball players who drew top competition from throughout the southland to City Stadium. Their captain, former San Diego High star Emmet Leighninger, boasted that they would be good. From April into September, the Bee Gees went undefeated against clubs from San Bernardino, Los Angeles, and Fullerton.

On September 12, Desmond's Blue Beauties, the top-ranked team in Los Angeles, came to town and beat the San Diegos, 4-1. The boys rebounded in October to defeat the United States amateur champions, White Auto of Cleveland, 5-4. The Bee Gees final record was 26-4. It was announced they would sport new threads in the winter league. They had previously worn the old Bears uniforms with "San Diego" in block letters. Their jerseys would feature "CCC" across the chests to reflect the name of their new sponsor: the Cabrillo Commercial Club. In those days the lines between professional and amateur status were often blurred. It was acceptable to pay players, but they could not be under contract to a professional baseball club.

Since the left field foul pole was only 247 feet away, a tall outfield fence was proposed at City Stadium to prevent cheap home runs. This was during the "Deadball Era," when by regulation foul lines only had to be 235 feet. With the advent of the "Lively Ball Era" in 1920, this short left field porch in San Diego's primary ballpark would make it difficult to get a professional baseball team.

That same year, Gavy Cravath, San Diego's first major leaguer, established the modern major league season home run record when he slugged 24 round-trippers for the National League champion Philadelphia Phillies. Cravath, a right-handed power hitter, had become expert at clearing the 30-foot Baker Bowl wall in right field, where it was only 279 feet down the line.

Albert B. Spalding died on September 9, 1915. Prior to his death, the future Hall of Famer had engaged harbor engineer John Flynn to acquire over 1,000 acres of tideland property, in an area known as Dutch Flats, for the purposes of creating a great naval base in San Diego. A seawall was eventually built and the bay was dredged to backfill the mud flats to a height of six feet above sea level. The original project was to run from F Street to Hawthorn Street. The headquarters building for the Eleventh Naval District and the San Diego County Administrative Center are currently located on this reclaimed land. Spalding would have been pleased to know that Lane Field, the original home of the San Diego Padres, would rise on the bayfront at the foot of Broadway.

The Firemen played the Police for comic relief. Numerous prizes were donated by San Diego merchants. Sam Price of Price Clothing Company promised a suit to anyone hitting a ball over the centerfield bleachers. A modern chemical "firefighting" truck was offered to the fireman who would hit a home run with five men on base. Both teams reportedly enjoyed a "champagne bath" the night before the game. No doubt both sides bathed in the bubbly after the game as well.

A shortened Southern California Professional League schedule ran from November 6 though December 5. Will Palmer's aggregation of familiar faces would now be called the Pantages. They started impressively with a couple of victories over Rube Foster's Chicago American Giants. Roy "Hippo" Hitt still had enough magic in his "good old soupbone" to claim the opener, 7-4. The next day, Cincinnati's Pete Schneider pitched and batted the Pantages to a 6-2 triumph against the Giants.

The results were different the next time the teams tangled. Frank "The Red Ant" Wickware spun a one-hit, 4-0 shutout on Thanksgiving Day, and the Giants squeezed past the Pantages in the second game, 3-2. San Diego came back to win the Sunday contest, 4-2, sparked by a Dick Bayless triple. The Pantages had planned to unfurl the championship pennant, but disaster stuck. The headlines read, "Chech Hurls No-Hit Game Shutting Out Palmer's Pets." San Bernardino's 36-year-old Charlie Chech, a big league veteran, stunned Palmer's nine on December 5, 6-0.

Later that month, the American Giants visited San Diego to pick up a little holiday cash and sweep a two game series. Bitter feelings had been festering on both sides. The "colored attitude" was described as "cocky" and "peevish." The second game almost got out of hand "when Wickware became too boisterous in his actions. Umps (sic) Chandler found it necessary to gently remonstrate with the Giants hurler by placing his open hand on Wickware's vocal outlet and tenderly shove him back some five or six feet." Chandler was credited with preventing "open warfare" and hostilities comparable "with those now being carried on by the belligerents in Europe." Because the locals came out on the losing end, there was none of the sportsmanship shown in 1913.

San Diego hired Charlie Chech from San Bernardino to salvage the last game, but the Giants won, 3-2. This was an exceptional baseball team that featured such stars as John Henry "Pop" Lloyd, Pete Hill, Bruce Petway, Frank Duncan, Dizzy Dismukes, Joe Williams and, of course, Frank Wickware. Foster's black American Giants officially won the California Winter League for the first time, which caused problems. This was an era when players did not fraternize with opponents regardless of race, so both sides contributed to ill feelings. It was easier for whites to be gracious when they won.

Amateur ball was enjoying unprecedented success throughout the county in 1916. Games were now being played at City Stadium, Athletic Park, Golden Hill, Chollas Valley, the Army Base, El Cajon, Old Town, and across from the Fire Station at Eighth and J Streets. The San Diego County Managers Association was formed to govern local baseball and the top teams included the Cabrillo Club, the Hippodromes, PM Dairy and the US Marines. The City League, formed in April of 1916, dissolved in June when PM Dairy players (workers) had given up the sport during "the press of business during the summer months." The Milkmen had an impressive 23-7 record when they went into retirement.

East San Diego was using a 14-year-old pitcher named Earle Brucker. Benefit games with all proceeds going to Arthur King, a disabled player, would continue for several years. The Bankers League, Trolley League, military, and independent teams were thriving. Junior baseball shared the spotlight. Five hundred fans watched the Cycle & Arms Juniors take the league championship from Golden Hill at the Firemen's grounds.

A new town team, appropriately known as San Diego, was assembled by former Cabrillo manager OJ Hull. True to script, they beat up on all the best teams of Southern California, including Riverside, which listed several famous members from the legendary Carlisle Indians baseball team. Their catcher was a Native American known only as Jim. Could his last name have been Thorpe? Pacific Light and Power, numero uno among white teams in Los Angeles, proved better than Hull's boys. The high point of the season was splitting four games with the colored Los Angeles White Sox. Their star pitcher, "Moonshine" Mooney, threw underhand. The Sox grew into an African American institution in LA and continued to play into the 1950s.

On December 2, the Logan All-Stars buried Cycle & Arms, 17-5. By popular vote, Charles

Stradley was deposed as C&A manager and replaced by outfielder Carl Klindt. The youthful new skipper would exercise major influence over San Diego baseball for the next three decades.

The Cabrillos assumed the mantle of the Pantages in the winter league and continued in their winning ways. North Park won the 1916–1917 Trolley League by beating the Hippodromes. William Wilson, "a grammar school Christy Mathewson," pitched Logan School to the city championship in March with a 1-0 gem against Sherman. While Wilson was fanning 11 Shermans, Clarence Maggarell, "a young Walter Johnson," whiffed 15 Logan batters.

San Diego High School won the Southern California football championship during the autumn of 1916. The Hillers also captured the 1917 Southland baseball title with a decisive 12-2 triumph over Norwalk. Future San Diego Police Chief Wesley Sharp led all hitters with a .412 batting average. With an enrollment of 2,000 and a first class stadium, San Diego High School's athletic program was gaining national recognition

By the time America entered the First World War in April 1917, summertime baseball had finally become the norm in San Diego. Travel was greatly curtailed, so the Pantages remained in town as the dominant team in the new Exposition Post League. Cycle & Arms won the Trolley League. Several new service teams emerged, among them were the Machine Gun Company, the Second California Regiment, the Ambulance Corps, the Utah Field Artillery, Camp Kearny, Naval Aviation, the 115th Sanitary Train, Fort Rosecrans, Torpedo Reserves, Army Company M, Company K, Companies 13–18, Navy Firemen, and numerous Navy ship teams: the USS Maryland, USS Oregon, USS Minneapolis, USS Pittsburg (sic), USS Whipple and the USS Alert.

At the end of the 1917 season, San Diego Sun sportswriter Paul Purman began an article, "Who is the hardest hitter in baseball today?" The first name on his list was Gavvy Cravath. (Sportswriters added the extra "v" to rhyme with "savvy.") Purman concluded that Babe Ruth was the hardest hitter. Ruth had just finished a 24-13 year on the mound, but he also hit 11 home runs in only 317 times at-bat to lead the AL. Although the sportswriter had inflated some of Babe's batting figures to make his point, he was on to something. Among other things, the fans loved Ruth.

Service base ball was now the main game in San Diego. The Army's 3-0 shutout of Navy in February of 1918 was described as "one of the best games ever played in San Diego." A month later, the sailors split a two-game series with the Los Angeles Angels.

San Diego High School won the state base ball championship with a 2-1 victory over Sacramento. Future major leaguer Frank "Stubby" Mack struck out seven Dragon batsmen and allowed four hits as the Hilltoppers won their first state championship in any sport. On May 13, 1918, former San Diego High School athlete and assistant coach Ralph N. Noble was killed in action during "the Great War."

The Fire Department was San Diego's top civilian team in 1918. The Firemen met the Navy in Balboa Stadium on February 23, 1919, for the final game of the season. Two thousand spectators watched Jack Ryan and his fire-fighting teammates hold off the Tars, 5-3. Ryan was known for "mixing up his 'mudder' with his shoulder ball."

In April of 1919, Jack Bryan began writing a column in the San Diego Sun known as "Just Baseball." He chronicled the early history of base ball in San Diego, but quickly ran out of material. That summer, several leagues formed. East San Diego, the Gas Company, San Diego Fire, Camp Kearny, and the Shipyard were considered the cream of the crop. Three thousand and five hundred fans watched Tom Downey's Shipyard team win the city title from the Firemen, 6-2. There were complaints from those who wanted "clean sport" about Downey's professional ringers. It was unclear if the fans opposed this practice. Was it the Firemen? Perhaps the most complaints came from the San Diego Sun sportswriters.

A week later, the Shipyards swamped the Los Angeles champion Dyas, 10-1, at City Stadium before 4,500 cheering fans. Downey's crew also beat, in succession, Wade "Red" Killifer's All-Stars, Casey Stengel's All-Stars, and Carl Sawyer's San Pedro nine.

"A comet swerved from its orbit yesterday long enough to raise the blood pressure of 4,659 rabid fans to the danger zone when 'Babe' Ruth with eight lesser meteorites, outshone old Sol for a couple of hours." The Shipyards met their match when the Babe Ruth All-Stars came to town on December 28, 1919. The Great Bambino went 3 for 6, including a mighty home run in a decisive 15-7 victory over San Diego. During batting practice, Babe drove at least three balls between the columns at the south end of the stadium. As the stories grew, legend has it that one of the balls rolled all the way to Broadway . . . a memorable ending to another colorful decade of base ball in San Diego.

FIELD DAY AT ATHLETIC PARK. San Diego school children enjoyed a day of track and field activities at Athletic Park on May 14, 1910. This ballpark, which opened in November of 1906, was located at Twenty-Sixth (Sampson) and Main Streets. (Courtesy San Diego Historical Society, SDHS #88:16525)

ALBERT G. SPALDING. Al Spalding helped organize the National League in 1876. He pitched the Chicago White Stockings (Cubs) to the league's first title with a 47-13 record. In 1901, the recently widowed founder of AG Spalding Sporting Goods married his mistress, Elizabeth Churchill, and moved to San Diego.

THE SLUGGERS, 1911. These sturdy young lads were known as the Sluggers base ball team. This picture was taken in Balboa Park. (Courtesy San Diego Historical Society, SDHS #91:18564-2215)

THE SAN DIEGO BEARS. The original San Diego Bears were organized by Will Palmer in 1911. The team started slowly, but reeled off 16 straight victories and coasted to the Southern California championship. "Bears" was a popular and common team name in the early 1900s because the grizzly bear, featured prominently on the California flag, is the state symbol. (Courtesy San Diego Historical Society, SDHS #14685)

1911 CHAMPIONS OF THE CALIFORNIA WINTER LEAGUE. (Courtesy Tom Larwin)

SLIM NELSON. Harry Nelson was born in Batavia, Illinois, in 1884. Although one of the Coast League's top pitchers in 1910, he landed in San Diego, "on vacation," in June of 1911. The Gas Company inserted the calorie-challenged veteran into one of their baggy uniforms with hopes he could still baffle the locals with his assortment of "shoots and benders." Friends called him "Slim," but a sportswriter named him "Six O'clock," because he resembled the hands of a clock at that hour. In 1908, Slim threw a no-hitter against Oakland in the outlaw California State League. The only run of the game came on Slim's home run that went down a gopher hole. Nelson circled the bases as the outfielder tried in vain to retrieve the horsehide. He arrived in San Diego with "his wing needing a rest." That is exactly what it got. Old Six O'clock returned to Oakland with his "fine wife, excellent-looking daughter and a fine son, built along the lines of Slim."

WILLIAM "HEINIE" HEITMULLER. Under tragic circumstances, Heinie Heitmuller won the 1912 Pacific Coast League batting title with a .335 batting average—even though he was dead. The likable Los Angeles outfielder apparently contracted typhoid fever from his roommate, Hugh Smith, but continued to play. While deathly ill, he actually raised his batting average until Angels manager "Pop" Dillon was forced to remove him from the lineup. Another teammate, "Pete" Daley took over the lead in the batting race, but faltered in the last days and ended up at .332. Because of disease, death, even for healthy young ballplayers, was not uncommon. Benefit games would be held with gate receipts going to the family. Today, we take good health for granted.

OLD TOWN TEAM. This image was featured in the *San Diego Sun*, August 14, 1912. (Courtesy San Diego Historical Society, SDHS #20613)

SAFE AT THIRD. A runner slides in a cloud of dust to evade the tag as the Old Town pitcher backs up third base. (Courtesy San Diego Historical Society, SDHS #20614)

SAN DIEGO WATCHES THE WORLD SERIES. Fans "watch" the 1912 World Series on the Playograph outside the San Diego Sun office at the corner of Sixth and "B" Streets on October 15, 1912. (Courtesy San Diego Historical Society, SDHS #15747)

NATIONAL CITY HIGH SCHOOL TEAM, 1913. These National City boys were a perfect 6-0 in 1913. Pictured, from left to right, are Arnold Sheiniger, Blair Cantwell, John Gardner, Harold Vanderipe, Harry Kraft, Charles Willoughby, Louis Leffert, Elbert Crumley, Elden Pecka, George Wilfley, and Bennett S. Hale (coach). (Courtesy San Diego Historical Society, SDHS #12015)

RUBE FOSTER'S CHICAGO AMERICAN GIANTS. These *San Diego Union* cartoons, unacceptable by today's standards, were typical of the era. That "colored base ball" received any coverage in a white newspaper was unusual for the times. What is significant, however, is that the racist cartoons stopped as the sportswriters and fans grew to appreciate the talent and sportsmanship of Foster's American Giants.

Mr. Wilson, San Diego Bears Professional Base Ball Team. This is the only known photograph of a player in a San Diego Bears uniform (navy blue with white trim). Although Wilson's first name is unknown, we do know that he was from Salt Lake and swung a left-handed bat. The only connection this team had with the original Bears was their name. (Courtesy San Diego Historical Society, SDHS #12605-1)

Coffey, San Diego's Best Batter, Crossing Plate After He Drove Sphere Over Fence

Give That Man a Cigar. Centerfielder Coffey was given "a box of cigars, bottle of hair tonic, twenty free shines, a dozen street car tickets and a trip to Ta Juana (sic)" for hitting the Bears' first home run on Opening Day, April 22, 1913. These Bears were San Diego's first true professional team in the ill-fated Class D Southern California League. The circuit folded in July and San Diego was declared league champions. Team owner Dick Cooley would complain bitterly, "I can't understand the people, and I don't believe they'll make baseball pay here in a thousand years. I'm convinced they don't want baseball in San Diego."

CHARLES TOWNSLEY. Charlie Townsley was a pitcher for the Bears. This picture was taken on April 18, 1913. It appears that Townsley is wearing a San Diego road uniform with a script "S" on the left breast. (Courtesy San Diego Historical Society, SDHS #15737)

NEW YORK GIANTS VS. CHICAGO WHITE SOX IN SAN DIEGO. John McGraw and Charles Comiskey made San Diego one of the stops on their 1913 worldwide tour to promote base ball. Fans "kicked" when the game was called for darkness. Play resumed and Sox hurler "Death Valley Jim" Scott grooved the first pitch to Giants catcher Chief Meyers. "Scott glanced up, saw the sphere disappear in the region of the bay, and walked off the field." The locals went home feeling their money had been well spent. (Courtesy San Diego Historical Society, SDHS #1998/65.5)

A LITTLE CHIN MUSIC. Catcher Chief Meyers snags a high, inside pitch at Athletic Park for the Quality Brewery team. Bill Palmer had found a new sponsor and the San Diego Winter team was now known both as the Qualities and the Brewers. (Courtesy San Diego Historical Society, SDHS #20785)

SAN DIEGO AG SPALDING CHAMPIONS. Albert Spalding awarded plaques to a number of public school leagues across the country. The 1913 AG Spalding Champions were the Washington School in Oshkosh, Wisconsin, the Lamar School in Houston, the Northwest School in Hartford, Connecticut, and the Logan Heights School in San Diego.

CUYAMACA CLUB LAMBS. The bachelors, from left to right, are (front row) Bill Rife, Les Moon, Charles Williams, Doc Chamberlain, Clarence Sprigg, and Vic Morgan; (back row) Jim Tillmore, Tom Hammond, Charles Forward, and Lester Bradley. They faced a team of non-bachelors in February of 1914. (Courtesy San Diego Historical Society, SDHS #OP14713-1)

CUYAMACA CLUB GOATS. The married men, from left to right, are (front row) unknown, Alex Reynolds, Andy Ervast, HD Davis, J. Forward, and Chaffee Grande; (back row) George Parker, Frank Allen, Harry Jones, Milton Barber, Frank Turnbull, Jay Gould, Jerry Ingle, and Frank Reicher. The old Goats lost to the single guys, 13-9. (Courtesy San Diego Historical Society, SDHS #OP14713)

LAKESIDE TEAM, 1914. The Lakeside team included Jesse Brockley, Dan Marquis, Tex Zellner, Roy Rowe, Earl Zellner, Wallace Phillips, Joe Murillo, Earl Pratt, Vic St. Cyr, Clifford Gagne, and manager Guy Dort. Special excursion rates on the San Diego & South Eastern Railway took fans all the way to Lakeside for Sunday ball games. Stops included Encanto, Lemon Grove, La Mesa, El Cajon, Grossmont, and Santee. When communities along the rail lines played one another, they formed what were commonly known as "trolley leagues." (Courtesy San Diego Historical Society, SDHS #9663)

LEMON GROVE AND ENCANTO TEAMS, 1914. Trolley teams in Encanto and Lemon Grove enjoyed base ball in the wide open spaces. (Courtesy San Diego Historical Society, SDHS #18109-9-D)

ALL AMERICANS. Pictured, from left to right, are: (front row) Duffy Lewis, Luke Boone, Young Moriarty, Jimmy Walsh, McAvoy "Wickey" McAvoy, Danny Murphy, and "Bullet Joe" Bush; (back row) Ray Chapman, George Moriarty, Dick Hoblitzell, Ira Thomas, "Lefty" James, John Henry, and Willie Mitchell. These National League stars played an exhibition game against their American League counterparts on December 27, 1914. (Courtesy San Diego Historical Society, SDHS Palmer Collection Original)

ALL NATIONALS. Pictured, from left to right, are: (front row) Art Fletcher, "Dots" Miller, "Cozy" Dolan, Jeff Tesreau, Grover Cleveland Alexander, and Bobby Byrne; (back row) Max Carey, Fred Clarke, "Hippo" Vaughn, Dave Bancroft, Ed Burns, "Red" Killifer, Bill James, and Fred Snodgrass. Future Hall of Famer Alexander won for the Nationals, 1-0. (Courtesy San Diego Historical Society, SDHS Palmer Collection Original)

DUTCH TREAT FOR INDIANAPOLIS. Herman "Dutch" Bronkie waits for his pitch in a San Diego exhibition game between the American Association Indianapolis Indians and Coast League Venice Tigers on March 6, 1915. (Courtesy San Diego Historical Society, SDHS #UT7882)

TIGERS RALLY TO SCALP INDIANS. Tub Spencer connects as the Tigers scored two in the ninth inning to edge Indianapolis, 8-7. Catching for the Indians is Dick Gossett. (Courtesy San Diego Historical Society, SDHS #UT7883)

ONE OUT. Venice first sacker Charles "Swede" Risberg makes the put out as Chicago catcher Wally Mayer lumbers down the line in exhibition play at Athletic Park on March 8, 1915. (Courtesy San Diego Historical Society, SDHS #UT7894)

TWO OUT. Risberg won this race for the bag with his future White Sox teammate Oscar "Happy" Felsch. The Chicago centerfielder was out by a couple of steps. Six years later, both players would be out of baseball for their involvement in the Black Sox scandal. (Courtesy San Diego Historical Society, SDHS #UT7895)

CITY STADIUM (BALBOA STADIUM), 1915. City Stadium, "the greatest public playground in the United States," officially opened on May 31, 1915. The stately colonnade at the south end is seen in this picture of the Al Bahr Shrine and Golden Hill Playground teams. The left field

GAVY GRAVATH, HOME RUN KING. San Diego County's first major leaguer, Clifford Carlton Cravath, set a modern home run record when he pounded out 24 round-trippers for the Philadelphia Phillies in 1915. That year, Gavy hit as many or more home runs than 12 of the 15 other major league teams. The Phillies captured their first National League pennant in 1915 as Grover Cleveland Alexander won 31 games for the Quakers. When Cravath retired in 1920, he had also established a new career record with 119 home runs. It is interesting to note that in the 1915 World Series, the Boston Red Sox respected Cravath's right-handed power so much that they didn't use a brilliant young left-handed pitcher who had won 18 games that season. His name: Babe Ruth. Ironically, it would be the great Bambino who broke Gavy's season and career home run records.

fence offered a short shot into the stands, but it took a mighty blow to reach the columns in right. This magnificent facility was not known as Balboa Stadium until 1939. It was better suited for football and track. (Courtesy Rusty Hansen)

CARL KLINDT. Cycle & Arms had long been an innovative presence in San Diego league ball since the early 1900s, but C&A hit bottom during the winter of 1915. They acquired the strong right arm of star "pill tosser" Charles "Teedles" Stradley. The team rebounded to capture the fall title and the new pitcher took over the helm. Despite success on the field, the club became wracked with dissension. By popular vote, Charles Stradley was deposed as manager and replaced by first baseman/outfielder Carl Klindt. The youthful new skipper would prove to be a resourceful organizer and he would exercise major influence over San Diego baseball for the next three decades. It was important that Klindt could maintain balance between the factions who constantly fought about domination for amateur or professional baseball.

1916 TROLLEY LEAGUE RUNNER-UPS. The headline read, "Parks trounce Hipps for the Trolley Flag." This Hippodrome player looks like he might have been the losing pitcher in the title tilt won by North Park, 8-2. The boys in the back seat are pretty grim as well, but his wife looks ready for a Sunday ride in their fancy new automobile. (Courtesy San Diego Historical Society, SDHS #99:19906-25)

1917 STATE HIGH SCHOOL CHAMPIONS. The Hillers (not yet the Cavemen or even the Cavers) captured their second consecutive Southern California baseball title with a decisive 12-2 triumph over Norwalk. They are, from left to right, (front row) George Roberts, Clyde Warner, Walter "Dutch" Eels (captain), Alan Sampson, Clyde Randall, Paul Fields; Back row: Bryan Sprott (manager), Don Walters, Wes Sharp, Gene Butler, Nibs Price (coach), Edward Case, Thompson, Willie Devine.

USS ALERT BASE BALL TEAM. With the nation at war, service teams emerged in 1917. Ship teams included the mighty *USS Maryland, USS Oregon, USS Minneapolis, USS Pittsburgh, USS Whipple* and the little *USS Alert.* (Courtesy San Diego Historical Society, SDHS #7271)

ARMY-NAVY BALL AT THE STADIUM. This was another "one of the best games ever played in San Diego," when the soldiers beat the sailors, 3-0, in 12 innings at City Stadium on February 1, 1918. Hall (starter for Army) and Grimes (for Navy) dueled for 11 shutout innings until the Tars hurler was removed for a pinch runner. After his replacements loaded the bases, a blown double play spelled defeat for the valiant swabs. The Navy catcher in this picture is Arthur "Pops" Billings. (Courtesy San Diego Historical Society, SDHS #UT7881)

FIREMEN BASE BALL TEAM. The San Diego Fire Department boasted city's top civilian team in 1918. The Firemen met the Navy in Balboa Stadium on February 23, 1919, for the final game of the season. Two thousand spectators watched Jack Ryan and his fire fighter teammates hold off the Sailors, 5-3. Ryan was known for "mixing up his 'mudder' with his shoulder ball." (Courtesy San Diego Historical Society, SDHS #80:6666 detail)

THIRD ANNUAL BALL. This is the invitation to the popular benefit dance for San Diego Baseball that was held at the Dreamland Auditorium (First and A) on December 5, 1919. The proceeds from the ball were to be used by the local Class B and Class C amateur leagues. "The best union music that can be secured will be on hand to furnish the jazz. A grand time is promised for all those who attend." San Diego was ready for the "Roaring Twenties."

SIX

"Padres Beat San Diego"

1920–1929

San Diego Population: 74,683
Weather: Sunny, 72 degrees

Savage Tires won the 1920 Class B City Championship, but it was bigger news when the Babe Ruth All-Stars returned to City Stadium on January 18, 1920. Under hazy skies, Ralph Dawson's "shine ball looked weird" to Ruth and his mates, and the San Diego right-hander cooled the visitors' bats. Although Ruth collected two late-inning singles, the locals were on the long end of the 4-2 score. Dawson could brag that he struck out Babe Ruth. None of the 3,270 fans requested a refund.

That same weekend, the San Pedro Sub Base team flew by airplane to San Diego for a game with Pacific Fleet Air Detachment. "Sunny Jim" Coffroth, operator of the Calienta Racetrack in Tijuana, contacted William McCarthy, president of the Pacific Coast League, about the possibility of San Diego landing a team "in the next couple of years." McCarthy suggested that perhaps the Northwest teams could play their early and late season games in San Diego "to test the San Diego enthusiasm." Neither this plan nor expansion to include San Diego and Vancouver were taken serious. San Diego did succeed in winning the Southern California League championship with a 2-1 win over Carl Sawyer's San Pedro All-Stars on February 29, 1920.

The famous Boston Bloomer Girls came to San Diego on March 14, 1920, and lost a 4-3 contest to the Chief Meyers All-Stars. Talk renewed to move Bill Lane's Salt Lake City team to San Diego as the Coast League opener loomed. The town team beat the PCL Venice Tigers 14-4 on March 28, 1920. A visitor to San Diego observed, "All they seem to do around this town is play baseball."

Fort Rosecrans won the 1920 Southern California Army Baseball championship. The San Diego Reserve Destroyers won the Pacific Fleet championship by taking a three game series from the USS Arkansas. The last game drew 15,000 fans—"the majority gobs"—to City Stadium as the Destroyers sank the big guns of the Arkansas, 13-5. By virtue of a 5-3 triumph over Alameda High, San Diego High School reigned again as 1920 State Baseball Champions.

In September, a bitter dispute erupted between proponents of local league ball and Southern California Winter League baseball. Tom Downey's supporters wanted a single strong team to take on all comers each Sunday at the stadium. The Gas Company, Firemen, Standard Oilers, and Naval Air Station all wanted to use City Stadium for their own league play. A vote was taken by the local newspapers and the pros claimed a narrow victory. A compromise was reached with the professionals and the four-club league sharing the bowl on Saturdays and Sundays.

The Vernon Tigers came to the stadium on November 21, 1920. Five thousand curious fans turned out to watch San Diego, with Chicago Cubs hurler Elwood "Speed" Martin on the mound, shut out the Coast Leaguers, 8-0. Patrolling centerfield, San Diego had the one and only Ty Cobb. The Georgia Peach even stole home in the third inning and pitched in the ninth to preserve Speed's white wash. The Tigers reliever Nick Altrock stuck out Martin. When asked the secret of his success, Altrock shrugged, "Drink fifty bottles of two per cent and get a hundred per cent proof."

A team known as Alexander's Colored Giants lost three straight to San Diego in the Southern California Winter League. Ballparks were scarce in Los Angeles, so San Diego did not have to travel. Apparently the LA teams grew weary of losing in San Diego and stopped coming southward. On January 30, 1921, a benefit game was scheduled between the Pacific Fleet and Carl Klindt's Cycle & Arms club. The Navy recruited the great Grover Cleveland Alexander to face his Cubs teammate and friend, Speed Martin. Alexander struck out Martin in the seventh, but the catcher dropped the ball. Speed circled the bases when "rank throws by the first and third basemen enabled him to make the round trip." C&A won, 3-2.

When the pros left for spring training, attention shifted to service ball and local league play. The Firemen cinched the City League "bunting" while the Naval Air Station took three straight from the USS Charleston to claim the Service League title.

After San Diego High School won the state baseball championship for the third time in four years, a series was arranged at City Stadium with Eastern powerhouse, undefeated West Tech of Cleveland. In the first game, a crowd of 12,000 cheered as the Hilltoppers slammed Tech, 10-0. Two days later on the Fourth of July, San Diego earned the national championship by edging the visitors, 7-6, in 10 innings.

General Rodriguez, commander of "Lower California [armed] forces," reportedly had a good baseball team. "Rodriguez, himself, is some player and one of the best third sackers in this part of the country." His ambitious plan to play Coast League teams after the season drew yawns. Such bravado was common on both sides of the border.

San Diego had a new town team called the Balboa Parks. The players were former San Diego High stars and their pitcher was Hilltoppers coach John Perry. They did well against semi-pro Los Angeles area teams. They finally lost to an LA team on October 9, 1921. It was the Coast League Angels who beat them, 4-3. Back in San Diego, La Mesa won the County championship and boldly challenged the Balboas to a game. Both teams brought in Navy pitchers and Balboa Park was lucky to squeak out a 1-0 victory to avoid the embarrassment of losing to a "league team."

A new idea to promote interest (attendance) gave fans the opportunity to vote for an all-star team to tackle the Balboa Park Club. The concept was an unqualified success. On May 7, 1922, the "largest crowd that has attended a Sunday baseball game in the city stadium this year" turned out to watch the Balboas prevail, 2-1, on a suicide bunt in the bottom of the ninth. A week later, the Parkers easily beat the All-Stars, 6-2. Since it was summer, the Balboas joined and dominated the Class A County League. The San Diego Rowing Club won the Saturday PM League and Escondido's Odd Fellows Lodge captured the North County Valley League flag.

San Diego High was severely penalized by the Southern California Interscholastic Federation for participation in the so-called 1921 national championship series with Cleveland. For punishment, the Hilltoppers were not allowed to compete against high school teams in 1922. Undaunted, coach Perry's boys finished the year 8-4 against top military and college teams that included UCLA and Stanford. Somehow West Tech arranged a rematch and the Hilltoppers again prevailed, 6-0 and 7-0. San Diego High School made a lot of money by hosting these games. Perhaps they shared the bread with the SCIF this time because they were again able to schedule high school games in 1923.

Another variation of Money Ball was promoted when the Navy All-Stars met Johnny Lambert's picked civilian team at the stadium in August of 1922. All proceeds were earmarked for the "Millan-for-State-Treasure" campaign war chest. "As president of several baseball leagues, he [Jack Miller] stood for clean sports, and ruled the ball players with an iron hand in this respect." Tickets sold "like hot cakes."

In September of 1922, a serious effort was made to organize an eight-team, Class B professional baseball league in Southern California. Will Palmer was asked to invest in the proposed San Diego franchise. The crusty old Pickwick manager held out for a Coast League team. Although the new league failed to get off the ground, Palmer reemerged as a force on the local baseball scene. He bitterly attacked the Park Board for "stalling" when he tried to get San Diego back into the Southern California Winter League. "Last year they experimented with the local talent and the season was a miserable [financial] failure."

Harry Jacob's Balboa Park team proudly represented San Diego during the 1922–1923 winter season. Tex Marley, Jack Killeen, and former San Diego High School hurlers Stubby Mack and Willie Praul shared mound duties for the Balboas. Their battery mate was Earle Brucker. They claimed impressive victories over the Vernon Tigers, Pirrone All-Stars, and Kansas City Monarchs. It is possible that local papers thought KC was the opposition when San Diego was actually playing the Winter League champions, the black LA White Sox. Jacob's team did not complete their full road schedule which would indicate they did not make enough money to cover expenses.

On May 20, 1923, a group of Spanish-American War veterans played a game of vintage base ball with 1890 rules during their "annual campfire picnic" in Balboa Park. They were the only rules the umpire knew. The final score was 44-44. That same day, the San Diego Goofs, wearing new uniforms, zipped the Temecula Indians, 11-0, at Murietta Hot Springs. Rumors persisted that "those in the know" would form a Class B league. Nothing happened. San Diego High School, now nicknamed the Cavemen, muscled another Southern California baseball championship.

On July 6, 1923, the San Diego Baseball Manager's Association was formed in an attempt to hold teams to a schedule. In the past, if a team failed to appear for a game, nothing could be done to penalize the offenders. Transportation expenses were often a problem, but player "jumping" (switching teams) was never addressed.

Chuck Willoughby's National City team won the County League title. Memorial Playground, with 16-year-old pitching whiz Gook Nielsen blazing the way, took the City League. The Telephone Company beat the Rowing Club in the Commercial League. First National Bank and Bank of Italy met in a three game championship series for the Bank League crown. Each team "obtained" a top pitcher from higher league teams. Do you suppose they received free checking or a set of steak knives for their services?

Fleet Air (winners of the Service League) and the Firemen (City League champs) split a two game series at the stadium. The Fliers won the first game, 4-1. "Tex was at his best pitching against his former teammates of the Fireman club and while he may have used licorice, talcum, emery, sticky flypaper, and a bit of mud on the seams, it must be admitted that Marley 'doped' the ball in clever fashion, and also that he pitched a super article of baseball." Was Marley a fireman or a swab? Who cares? The Firemen won the second game, 5-1, and the privilege to face off with the Buick Auto Nine, Los Angeles Exposition Park League champions. The Buicks won, 2-1, and made the mistake of thinking they could also defeat a team of San Diego All-Stars over Labor Day weekend.

The Stars smashed the northerners, 9-3 and 13-1, but was their decision to play in San Diego a mistake? The Buicks had a guaranteed purse of $200. Victorious local promoter Harry Jacobs ended up losing $21.75. He complained "that fans having proved by their failure to turn out at the bowl yesterday and Sunday that they prefer the local brand of baseball."

A month later, Jacobs reconsidered and assembled a strong club to wear "brand new uniforms with the words San Diego in large letters." He signed only professional players and immediately began knocking off the top LA teams (Pirrone's All-Stars, Bodie's All-Stars, Hammond Lumber, White King Soap), whose rosters included such stars as Babe Herman, Ping Bodie, Pete Schneider, and future Padres manager, spitballing Frank Shellenback. The final standings of the 1923–24 California Winter League standings are incomplete, but the colored Stars of St. Louis have been recognized as the champions. It appears that Jacobs' team won four of the five games played against St. Louis in San Diego, which may not have been taken into account in the standings.

Of note, on December 3, 1923, San Diego nailed Cool Papa Bell, a man so fast "that he could snap off the light, get into bed, and pull the covers up before the room went dark." On this occasion, outfielder Harry Courtney robbed the Stars' Bill Riggins of extra bases with a spectacular catch. "Recovering his balance he shot the ball to Ramage, who relayed quickly to Roche at first to double out Bell. The drive looked like a sure hit and Bell was racing around the bases, bent on scoring."

Logan Heights Athletic Club won the 1924 Winter County Championship behind the clever pitching slants of "Lefty" Gook Nielsen. Wielding potent lumber for the Logan nine in the critical title series with Ocean Beach were future Wesley Sharp and the Pappert brothers, Phil and Dib.

The big news of the high school season was Sweetwater Union High School's 4-3 upset of San Diego High in a SCIF playoff game to crush the Cavemen's chances for yet another state championship. The irony is that earlier in the year, the San Diego jayvee had beaten these same Sweeties. It was the first time Sweetwater had ever won from a Hilltop nine. In a scheduling fluke, San Diego went on to sweep three games with the Tucson Badgers, Arizona State Champions and regarded as one of the best high school teams in America.

The San Diego Electric Railway Giants took the Summer County League crown with a 3-2 victory over a solid Richards & Bowman Ford team from National City. Speed Martin and Dean Coombs rotated on the mound for SDERY. Cy Ramage played first base for the Electrics. His brother Bill Ramage was the shortstop for National City. A third brother, Lee, was a boxer who fought future heavyweight champion Joe Louis in 1934 and again in 1935.

Chollas Valley beat Golden Hill for the Fall County League title. Year-around baseball had become so popular that the County Managers Association added three more circuits in 1925. There were now six leagues in San Diego; the established County, Central and Independent Leagues were joined by the new Federal, Industrial and Commercial Leagues. Efforts to restart baseball at San Diego State College were for naught. The *San Diego Sun* even sponsored the city's first youth league for boys under the age of 14. The Neighbor House juniors received brand new red and white uniforms from their coach, Bill Breitenstein.

The sports pages were full of local sandlot results: Golden Hill 7, Powell Motors 0; Memorial 6, University Tigers 5; City OD 8, Chollas Valley 13; North Park 12, San Diego and Arizona Railroad 1; G.H. Blues 16, U.S.S. Omaha 3; Neighborhood House 6, Chula Vista 5; General Tires 2, Richards & Bowman 3; Showley Brothers 4, *USS Chase* 2; Gasco 22, Brunswig Drug 4; Marines 3, 11th Squadron 0; Naval Air 13, U.S.S. Decatur 4; *USS Omaha* 4, University Heights 7; Santa Ana Knights of Columbus 3, San Diego Knights of Columbus 4; Brunswig Drug 6, Encanto 7; Benson Lumber 13, American Express 16; Maydole-Smith 5, University Heights 3; Standard Iron 9, Campbell Chevrolet 15; Glasson Planing 1, GH Reds 15; L&W 6, Memorial 7. Not all games were reported.

Linn Platner's General Tire was the new class of San Diego sandlot ball. In early January, the Tires took a pair of games from Southern California Winter League powerhouse Gilmore Oil of Los Angeles. Although the Chula Vista Browns had won the local winter championship, General Tire took the County League pennant from the Brownies on June 28, 1925. Memorial Junior High School demoralized Golden Hill, 19-2, in the junior championship game. The hot rumor in town was that Bill Lane's Salt Lake team would move "if it [San Diego] has the money."

On September 5, 1925, the *Sun* announced that in addition to the General Tire-San Diego Colored Giants and *USS Nitro*-Western Metal baseball games, the first San Diego surf board meet would take place at Mission Beach. On September 7, life-guard Charles Wright skillfully rode his 9-1/2 foot, 130-pound board to victory. He was proclaimed the Pacific Coast Champion and given a miniature gold surf board.

The *San Diego Sun* "installed the latest improved mechanical device, the 1925 model 'Playograph," for fans to enjoy the World Series outside their office at the corner of Seventh and "B" Streets. "The Playograph actually plays the game and leaves nothing to the imagination. It is imposing in size and appearance, readable from a distance and as clear to understand as a first grade reader. The latest technology included 'the moving ball.'" Traffic jams, cheering, and horn blowing were reported throughout the series.

Neighborhood House met Encinitas in a crucial game. The beach boys only had seven players, so good sport Bill Breitenstein generously let them borrow Johnny Hernandez and Alfredo Vidal. Vidal collected four hits for Encinitas. NH had difficulty hitting the famous Hernandez curve and lost, 14-6. In another game, "The Opticians and Optometrists couldn't see the pill yesterday" and got beat by Silver Gate, 14-5.

The Chula Vista Browns, with future San Diego High School baseball coach Mike Morrow on the mound, captured the 1926 County Baseball Championship, 2-1, over the Optical All-Stars. The Opticals are not to be confused with the blind Opticians and Optometrists. San Diego State lost to the University of Southern California. Actually, it was the USC Dental College who drilled the Aztecs, 5-2. The PCL Salt Lake City Bees moved to Hollywood. San Diego had neither the money nor the ballpark necessary to land Bill Lane's team.

Harry Jacobs gathered San Diego's best ballplayers and arranged a four game series with Joe Pirrones Los Angeles All-Stars. Games would be held at the foot of Broadway in San Diego's newest enclosed ballpark, Navy Field. The Pirrones took the first pair of games, but San Diego came back to even the series. The new ballpark was shut down to add sod for future games that summer. San Diego would beat Pirrone's twice more in September when Navy Field was "made ready for the coming football season."

Facing Los Angeles Bank of Italy in an important inner-corporate clash, San Diego Bank of Italy decided to cook the books. Among the ringers they used were National City pitching wizard Chuck Willoughby. The local BIs won a pitcher's duel at City Stadium, 2-1. Future Padres owner C. Arnholt Smith, wittingly or unwittingly, played for this team.

At the the First Annual Ball Players Association golf tournament in Los Angeles, Speed Martin "nosed out" Arnold "Jigger" Statz to capture a silver loving cup. Charlie Chaplin, employing an unorthodox style, finished near the bottom of the winner's board.

San Diego State announced that Lee Waymire, former San Diego High assistant baseball coach, would take over the reigns of the young Aztecs baseball program.

The biggest news of 1927 was that Babe Ruth was coming to town again. On January 14, the Bambino would appear as himself in a contrived vaudeville act at the Pantages Theater. At the end of his performance, Babe would invite kids from the audience to join him on stage. He would ask them to sing, dance, or give a recitation. Then he would give each child an autographed baseball.

Everybody loved the routine . . . except the local state labor commissioner, a Mr. Stanley M. Gue, a bureaucrat's bureaucrat. He charged the Babe with willfully and unlawfully hiring a minor, Baby Annette deKirby, without a permit from the commissioner's office and for working said child, eight-years of age, "after the hour of ten PM," in violation of San Diego's strict curfew law.

In a detailed six-page opinion, the Honorable Claude L. Chambers determined that Babe Ruth was hardly running a sweat shop. The child in question was, after all, at the theater with her parents and her stage appearance clearly did not constitute employment. Babe was relieved when charges were dismissed. Coincidentally, little Annette deKirby, sister of future San Diego city councilman Ivor deKirby, had previously appeared with her brother in the popular "Our Gang" comedy series.

The House of David came to San Diego for a two-game series in March of 1927. These colorful barnstorming ballplayers with long hair and flowing beards were members of a religious sect out of Benton Harbor, Michigan. They practiced a healthy life style that included a vegetarian diet and rigorous physical exercise. "The Jesus Boys," as Satchel Paige called them, traveled across the country taking on all-comers and won 80 percent of their games. According to the *San Diego Sun*, the Davids had recently defeated Class A Dallas of the Texas League. The Texas team had just won the 1926 Dixie Series from Southern Association champs, New Orleans. House of David took the Saturday game, 3-1, and San Diego came back to win the Sunday tilt, 6-5. The House of David would play any on day of the week. They were spreading the gospel of baseball.

Harry Jacobs and his star pitcher Mike Morrow enjoyed great success against all Los Angeles teams except the Colored Giants. The teams split a series at Navy Field in May after San Diego had pounded LA clubs like Joe Pirrone's All-Stars (18-3) and Universal City (22-1). These teams played in the highly competitive Southern California Winter League. Sandlot leagues continued to flourish in San Diego with the University Grays capturing the County championship from Oceanside. Catcher Dallas Warren of Ryans Confectionery was developing a Babe Ruth reputation on San Diego sandlots. He hit a dozen home runs in 17 games.

The Pantages child labor misunderstanding did not deter the real Babe Ruth from a San Diego encore. Following his record-setting 60 home run season, Babe and Yankees teammate Lou Gehrig embarked on an ambitious barnstorming tour across America. Ruth would make $30,000 for his efforts, almost half of his regular season salary, and young Gehrig collected $10,000, which was two grand more than he made playing for New York that summer. On October 28, an estimated crowd of 3,500 turned out to watch the Bustin' Babes batter the Larrupin' Lous, 3-2, at Balboa Stadium. The teams were comprised of the top sandlotters in San Diego. Ruth and Gehrig each played first base for their respective sides. Though both demonstrated impressive power during batting practice, neither star homered during the game. Speed Martin pitched for his old friend's Bustin' Babes and Gook Nielsen tossed the pill for the Lous.

Although Baseball Commissioner Kenesaw Mountain Landis "banned colored winter baseball on the Coast," the threat proved unenforceable. Players from both races enjoyed sweet paydays under the warm California sun. The Philadelphia Royal Giants swept three games from San Diego in February of 1928. The following weekend, San Diego finally salvaged the last game of another three-game series, beating the Negro team, 9-7. The Royal Giants were a top ball team.

San Diego promoters attempted to persuade the Portland Beavers to play exhibition games at Navy Field. It was hoped the Portlanders would like San Diego so much they would abandon the rain for a permanent home in sunny San Diego.

San Diego State won two games and dropped four during the 1928 campaign. One of the victories was against Whittier, champions of the Southern California Collegiate League. It was the only loss the Poets would suffer that year.

Sandlot baseball continued to fill the sports pages. Bill Lane was having problems with his Los Angeles landlords. Angels owner William Wrigley insisted that women should be admitted free to his ballpark. Lane refused to follow this practice. Wrigley claimed the free admission cost him $29,000 in revenue, but he enjoyed granting free entry for ladies to Coast League games. When push came to shove, the League sided with Lane. The other owners lost money every time they came to Los Angeles, since the Wrigley largess for the ladies came right out of their share of gate receipts.

In January of 1929, something wonderful happened in San Diego. Hollywood owner Bill Lane pledged players, equipment, and $1,000 monthly stipend for a Class D professional baseball team in San Diego. The Stars would immediately move their spring training site to San

Diego. Bill Lane became an instant hero in San Diego. There was speculation that his Stars would also call San Diego home if a new ballpark could be built to league specifications. A Class D team was assured by February, but in early March, the courtship between Lane and San Diego suddenly went sour. The Hollywood owner had lost interest. The issue was pronounced dead.

In an abrupt turnabout, the newly organized California State League became reality by month's end. San Diego was awarded a franchise. CH "Doc" Atkins, former owner and manager of the Class A Denver team, and former big league catcher Sam Agnew were "the powers behind the guns." The Stars had released the 41-year-old Agnew to become skipper of the San Diego team. Home game would be played at Navy Field. A contest was held to name the team and, for unknown reasons, Aces was selected. Among the six who suggested the name was Escondido town team manager Alan "Dan" McGrew. San Bernardino decided to be called themselves the Padres.

On opening day, April 10, 1929, San Diego whipped San Bernardino, 9-6. Yes, San Diego beat the Padres! Orange County nipped the Bakersfield Bees, 7-6. It was noted that "Orange County did not look too hot in winning, but had the breaks." Ventura was supposed to be in the league. When the team could not secure a suitable ballpark, it was shuffled to the Orange County Fairgrounds.

By April 21st, the Aces were leading the league with a 9-3 record. It was clear that Atkins and Agnew had done a remarkable job filling the San Diego roster with quality players. Unwanted and unloved Orange County was struggling at 2-10. A week later, San Diego's lead over second place Bakersfield had increased to 4-1/2 games.

The Orangemen were barely competitive. On May 8, the Orange County team moved to the Los Angeles County Fairgrounds in Pomona. San Clemente was rumored to be the next stop. Six days later, "the fluttering butterfly" landed on a most unlikely flower: Coronado. With a sense of humor, the struggling franchise was appropriately renamed the Arabs. They would play at Navy Field until proper accommodations could be found on Coronado. The Aces were in first place with a 21-9 mark. San Diego County's second team, Coronado, was buried in the wine cellar at 6-24. The league was in trouble and so was Ace manager Sam Agnew. He had hit an umpire in Bakersfield and received a 10-day suspension.

Somehow Coronado began to win and San Diego began to lose. On June 11, it was reported that Fresno businessmen were interested in acquiring the improved Coronado team. A headline in the *San Diego Sun* on June 15 read, "Padres Beat San Diego 9 In 3rd Game." San Bernardino was now within a game of the first place Aces. On June 16, the Aces grabbed a Sunday doubleheader and the league's undisputed leadership at Navy Field. Coronado split a twin bill with the Bees in Bakersfield. A league meeting was held the next day at Los Angeles. Josh Clarke, president of the Bakersfield club, threw a bean ball. He withdrew his team from the league. Formal notification was sent to the National Association of Baseball Clubs. "Dear Sir: Have closed California State league season and first half, June 16, 1929, play to continue in 1930. Pennant awarded San Diego. Signed Harry Defty, president."

Rumors began to circulate that Hollywood, Portland, and Seattle were all anxious to move south. Ironically, the issue was clouded because the Aces held the territorial rights to San Diego.

Tryouts were announced for "all San Diego boys who will be under 17 years of age by Sept. 15" to join Mike Morrow's American Legion team. The San Diegans blasted La Jolla, 26-0, and La Mesa, 25-0. Tony Galasso threw a no-hitter in the second rout. Morrow's team was invited to the state tournament in Oakland. The Legionnaires, now wearing San Diego Aces uniforms, were loaded with power from San Diego High's SCIF championship team: Tony Galasso, Athos Sada, and the Holt twins, Roy and Ray. How good was that 1929 San Diego High School team? They lost a 7-6, 11-inning game to the Hollywood Stars rookies during spring training. Earlier that year in a game against Fullerton, Sada, the Holt boys and Alan Storton hit four consecutive home runs.

Before play could even begin, returning national champion Oakland successfully had Galasso declared ineligible on the basis of "professionalism and age." These charges were proven to be false. San Diego beat Long Beach, 8-2, and captured the state title with a thrilling, 12-inning, 3-2 victory over a surprise Mill Valley team that had upset Oakland the previous day.

As San Diego prepared to leave for the national tournament in Salt Lake City, an Oakland judge disqualified the team. It was learned that St. Augustine students, Pete Coscarart (Escondido HS) and Fred Traynor, had played for Morrow in the lop-sided victories over La Jolla and La Mesa. A Legion rule required that all players on a team had to attend the same high school.

Did San Diego have a reputation for cheating? It would be safe to say that rule manipulation, questionable player acquisitions, and deceit were common throughout baseball at that time. If deception worked, it was clever and accepted. An article appeared earlier that year about the time Wee Willie Keeler pretended to catch a game ending fly ball that disappeared into smoke that had blown across the field from a passing locomotive. The ball sailed over his head, but Keeler ran to the clubhouse like he had it in his glove. Baltimore won, 1-0. It was only cheating if it was detected.

Utilityman "Fat Boy" Johnnie Walters of San Diego was hailed as the Pacific Coast League's newest pitching sensation. San Francisco had given up on the overweight, error prone outfielder and traded him to Portland. The once proud Beavers had become the league's doormat. With rotund Walters on the mound, the team went on a 16-game winning streak to claim first place. "Junk" Walters, a product of San Diego sandlots, was a crowd favorite. The fans loved to laugh when he wobbled around the bases. He finished the season with a 12-5 record, 13 homers, and a .304 batting average. Unfortunately, the Beavers started to lose and sank to fourth place.

The Philadelphia Athletics won the 1929 World Series. Many believe this was the greatest baseball team of all time, even better than the 1927 Yankees. Hoping to cash in on the popularity of the 1927 Ruth-Gehrig barnstorming trip, Jimmie Foxx and Al Simmons duplicated their tour. The Philly stars performed before a small crowd at Balboa Stadium on October 30. Simmons slammed a couple of home runs into the stands while "Double X" and San Diego sandlotter Pete Grijalva each launched solo blows. In what seems to have been a tight game, the Foxx Sluggers beat the Simmons Aces, 7-6. The big leaguers also "tossed footballs with the high school varsity men and played ball on the side." It sounds like fun, but the game itself was described as poor and a farce. Was San Diego getting too sophisticated? Apparently Foxx and Simmons could not match Ruth and Gehrig in charisma.

Efforts to raise local sandlot baseball to a higher level were initiated and organizers began to charge twenty-five cents admission. The experiment did not prove successful. This was San Diego . . . a haven of cheapskates. The top sandlot teams in 1929 were the Gas Company, Western Dairies, the North Park Grays, Ryan's Confectioners, and George Harding's Colts. Showley Brothers Candy, the San Diego Electric Railway, and Marston's jockeyed for position in the Night Indoor League. Bill Lane continued to tease San Diego. The Chamber of Commerce kicked off a drive for a new ballpark. The nation was entering the Great Depression.

SAVAGE TIRE COMPANY. Savage Tires rolled to the 1920 Class B City Pennant. Team members included Aillaud, Pappert, Mundell, J. Pappert, Abell, Devine, Flynn, Wilson, Sharp, Baker. Their manager was Ralph Marshall. (Courtesy San Diego Historical Society, SDHS #S-282)

FORT ROSECRANS TEAM. The soldiers at Fort Rosecrans captured the 1920 Southern California Army Baseball championship. (Courtesy San Diego Historical Society, SDHS #S-502-2)

GAME ACTION AT SERVICE FIELD. Military baseball was very important in the 1920s. Games were played on reclaimed mud flats west of Pacific Boulevard near the former Middletown grounds. The approximate location of this diamond was on the current site of the County Administrative Center at 1600 Pacific Highway. (Courtesy San Diego Historical Society, SDHS #5776)

FORT ROSECRANS AND THE DOUGHBOYS. Not all of the Army clubs had fancy uniforms like the Fort Rosecrans team. This first baseman is wearing leather puttees. (Courtesy San Diego Historical Society, SDHS #5776-1)

GET BEHIND THE PLATE, UMP! The umpire positioned himself up the first base line to watch the slow trajectory of the left-hander's roundhouse curve. If it's not a "bender," that umpire would have been safer behind the catcher. San Diego Bay is seen in the background. (Courtesy San Diego Historical Society, SDHS #5776-2)

POP-UP. This swing may look like a home run over the A1 Flour Globe Mills grain elevators at Pacific and Beech, but the pitcher's head shows the ball was popped up instead. (Courtesy San Diego Historical Society, SDHS #5776-4)

"SERGEANT ROGERS MAKING A BIG SLIDE HOME." About all that needs to be said of this photo is that, hopefully, cups had been invented. To add insult to injury, it appears the sliding Camp Hearn cavalryman will be called out. (Courtesy San Diego Historical Society, SDHS #5776-3)

TY COBB IN SAN DIEGO. The Vernon Tigers came to town on November 21, 1920. Five thousand curious fans turned out to watch San Diego shut them out, 8-0, because patrolling centerfield for the locals was the one and only Ty Cobb. The Georgia Peach even stole home in the third inning. "Purposely walked in the third inning, Hannah's wide throw gave him second. He garnered third in neat fashion, and stole home in 'Big League' fashion. The ball thrown by Sawyer reached catcher Hannah's glove about the same time Cobb reached the plate, but Ty's base stealing education came to the fore, and he had a hand on the pan while Truck was trying to locate the world's greatest." Cobb even pitched in the ninth to preserve Speed Martin's white wash.

CYCLE & ARMS. Carl Klindt's Cycle & Arms team came from behind to sink the Pacific Fleet, 3-2, on January 30, 1921. Navy catcher Minor dropped a third strike and C&A pitcher "Speed" Martin took off for first base. "Rank throws by first and third basemen enabling him to make the round trip" to tie the score. Sanwick hit a "homer to the batting screen in centerfield" to win the game for the Klindts. (Courtesy San Diego Historical Society, SDHS #S-255)

ALEX THE SAILOR. Future Hall of Fame pitcher Grover Cleveland Alexander (third from left) was on the mound for the Pacific Fleet that day. The great right-hander was in town to visit his major league teammate and friend, Elwood "Speed" Martin (left). "Both he and Martin leave here in a couple of weeks for Murietta Hot Springs, where the Cub pitchers foregather."

YMCA FIELD. This view is looking north from the 11th Naval District Headquarters building at Broadway and Harbor Drive. Three baseball fields were located on this bayfront property now known as the North Embarcadero. The game being played in the middle of the picture was on the most popular field. A second layout can be seen in the lower right quarter and the third field is in the distance to the north. The right field line of the middle diamond would become the left field line at Lane Field in 1936. (Courtesy San Diego Historical Society, SDHS #7168-7)

FIRST PITCH AT YMCA FIELD. A naval officer fires a ceremonial opening pitch on the middle diamond at YMCA Field. Note the towers of the Santa Fe depot in left field. They were visible over the right field wall at Lane Field. (Courtesy San Diego Historical Society, SDHS #S-502)

CY HOMERS FOR THE *USS CHARLESTON*. This game was played on the southeast diamond at YMCA Field in 1921. The sailors watch along the first base line and Broadway in the roughly the same configuration as Lane Field. AS "Cy" Smith played catcher for one of the best Navy teams, the *USS Charleston*. Like so many other servicemen, he settled in San Diego.

PLAYING THE NATIONAL CHAMPIONSHIP SERIES FOR KEEPS. San Diego High School catcher Webster Gibson prepared to land on a flying Cleveland Techer at the plate. San Diego swept Cleveland Tech in a three game series at City Stadium for the national high school baseball title during the summer of 1921. More than 20,000 fans watched these battles.

BANK OF ITALY TEAM. One of the top teams in the 1923 Bankers League was Bank of Italy (later renamed Bank of America). How many recognize future Padres owner C. Arnholt Smith in the back row? Wearing his game face, Arnie stands third from left next to his happy manager.

SOUTHWESTERN BASEBALL. This was the most southwestern game of baseball ever played in the United States at Imperial Beach, California. It is not known if the Beachcombers ever used hand-me-down uniforms from the Bank of Italy. (Courtesy Chula Vista Heritage Museum)

SAN YSIDRO BEISBOL. Baseball was a hit in San Ysidro. Fans in their Sunday best watched games on the international border. (Courtesy Chula Vista Heritage Museum)

THE 1923 DURALITES. The Duralites were a mystery team that reportedly played in Chula Vista during 1923. At least one of their members appears to be a time-traveler from East San Diego. (Courtesy Chula Vista Heritage Museum)

HARTZELL'S GANG. Manager Bill Lackey assembled a fine La Mesa baseball team known as Hartzell's Gang. In one game, their battery was G. Serrano, T. Serrano, and D. Serrano. They should have been called Serrano's Gang. (Courtesy San Diego Historical Society, SDHS #87:16231)

SOUTHERN TRUST BANK TEAM. The only identified player in this 1923 photo of the Southern Trust team is Ole Rinde (far left, back row). Even with ringers like standout University of California hurler Gus Nemecheck, they finished the season in the accounts payable column. (Courtesy San Diego Historical Society, SDHS #89:17263)

SAN DIEGO ELECTRIC RAILWAY, 1924 COUNTY LEAGUE CHAMPIONS. The SDERY team defeated Richards & Bowman Ford of National City, 3-2, for the County title in 1924. Speed Martin registered victory for the Electrics. Each side had a Ramage son in the lineup. Their younger brother, Lee Ramage, would have two memorable fights with future heavyweight champion Joe Louis in 1934 and 1935. This photograph is probably from a later period, but 1924 was the finest hour for the Railway nine.

RICHARDS & BOWMAN FORD. The R&B boys were grim after losing the pennant to San Diego Electric Railway on August 3, 1924, at City Stadium. (Courtesy San Diego Historical Society, SDHS #OP14355)

NEIGHBORHOOD HOUSE. Neighborhood House always had good teams. Their players were primarily young Mexicans who lived where else . . . in the neighborhood. When NH met an Encinitas nine in a crucial game, the beach boys only had seven players. Good sport Bill Breitenstein generously let them borrow Johnny Hernandez and Alfredo Vidal. Vidal collected four hits for Encinitas and Neighborhood House hitters could not solve the famous Hernandez curve ball. Encinitas won, 14-6. (Courtesy Hernandez Family)

CHULA VISTA BROWNS, 1925 AND 1926 COUNTY LEAGUE WINNERS. The Chula Vista Browns defeated Neighborhood House, 2-1, for the 1925 San Diego County Championship. With future San Diego High School coaching legend Mike Morrow tossing a 2-1 victory in 1926, they repeated as county champs beating the Optical All-Stars. The champs, pictured from left to right, are (front row) Schaaf, Knutson, Foote, F. Schaaf, and Gibbons; (back row) Johnson, C. Smith, Kent, Morrow, Spencer, H. Smith, Dobranski, and their manager, Mr. C.V. Brown. (Courtesy Chula Vista Heritage Museum)

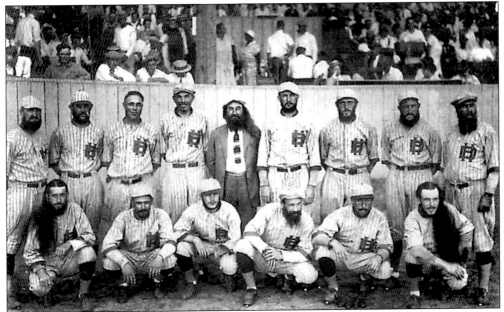

HOUSE OF DAVID. The House of David baseball Team came to San Diego for a two-game series in March of 1927. These colorful players with long hair and flowing beards were members of a religious sect. Satchel Paige called them "the Jesus Boys." House of David took the Saturday game, 3-1, but San Diego came back to win the Sunday tilt, 6-5. The Davids were barnstormers who spread the gospel of baseball. (Courtesy Terry Bertolino)

DUCK HUNTING WITH THE BABE. Babe Ruth takes a practice swing while duck hunting with Linn Platner at Sweetwater Reservoir on January 12, 1927. (Courtesy San Diego Historical Society, SDHS #UT3681)

BABE, CARL KLINDT, AND LOU GEHRIG. The Bustin' Babes and Larrupin' Lous arrived in town as part of an ambitious 1927 barnstorming tour across America. Ruth would make $30,000 for his efforts, almost half of his regular season salary, and young Gehrig collected ten grand, which was $2,000 more than he made playing for the Yankees that summer. Promoter Carl Klindt arranged the game at City Stadium. (Courtesy San Diego Historical Society, SDHS #UT3678)

BABE SWINGS AT BALBOA STADIUM. On October 28, 1927, an estimated crowd of 3,500 turned out to watch the Bustin' Babes bust the Larrupin' Lous, 3-2. The teams were comprised of the top sandlotters in San Diego. Ruth and Gehrig each played first base for their respective sides. Though both men put on an impressive slugging clinic during batting practice, neither homered in the game. (Courtesy San Diego Historical Society, SDHS #UT3680)

LOU GEHRIG. Pete Grijalva remembered the game well. "I hit a shot up the middle and I was thinking it was pretty good. I was on first and Gehrig said, 'Hey, kid, what the hell did you do? Hit that on your thumb?' I felt terrible. Then he smiled and tapped me on the head with his glove and said, 'Boy, you hit the hell out of that ball,' which made me feel pretty good." Grijalva never tired of telling people, "I played with the Babe. The thing I remember about Babe was a double play we made. A runner was on second and a ground ball went to our shortstop. He kind of bobbled it and Ruth had to stretch almost on his belly to catch it at first. Don't forget that he was left-handed, so the runner took off for third. Ruth just flipped a perfect strike to me and we had the guy by five feet. He just slid into the ball. Babe was nonchalant and made it look easy. For me, it was amazing. Babe Ruth was a phenomenal player." (Courtesy San Diego Historical Society, SDHS #OP15746-2625)

BABE AND THE KID. Billy Talbot, Gas Company mascot (bat boy), was the happiest kid in San Diego to be receiving batting tips from Babe Ruth. (Courtesy San Diego Historical Society, SDHS #UT3679)

ESCONDIDO BALL PARK. In the 1920s, the Escondido ball park was located at the corner of Escondido and San Diego Boulevards (Valley Parkway). They played night games with the aid of lights strung across the field. (Courtesy Escondido Historical Society, #5215)

I'VE GOT IT, I'VE GOT IT . . . YOU TAKE IT!!! How would you like to catch fly balls that went above the lights in night games at Escondido? (Courtesy Escondido Historical Society, #5216)

ESCONDIDO TOWN TEAM. Pictured, from left to right, are (front row) Rupert Baldridge, Felix Quisquis, Steve Coscarart, Lloyd Bagley, Dean Oliver, Marcus Alto, and Pete Coscarart; (back row) Ted Wright, Hal Finney, Joe Coscarart, "Lefty" Hunt, Sam Kolb, unknown, and Alan "Dan" McGrew. The Agnew-Lee-Agnew (ALA) Lumber Company is seen in the background. (Courtesy Escondido Historical Society, #5214)

THE SAN DIEGO MARINES. Lt. "Pop" Branch formed the Marine Corps Recruit Depot baseball team in 1928. The next year, Major Jay "Nig" Clarke, a former American League catcher with a 27-year career in baseball, returned to the Corps to take over the team. Clarke had served in the Marines during the First World War. This was the beginning of the rich MCRD baseball tradition that lasted into the 1960s. (Courtesy San Diego Historical Society, SDHS #UT7876)

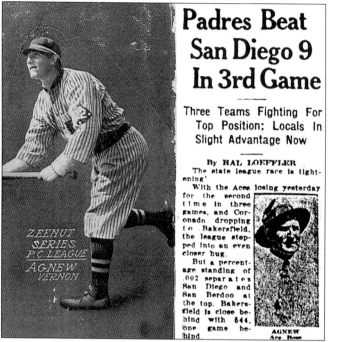

Padres Beat San Diego 9 In 3rd Game

Three Teams Fighting For Top Position; Locals In Slight Advantage Now

By HAL LOEFFLER

The state league race is tightening'

With the Aces losing yesterday for the second time in three games, and Coronado dropping to Bakersfield, the league stepped into an even closer hug.

But a percentage standing of .002 separates San Diego and San Berdoo at the top. Bakersfield is close behind with 644, one game behind.

AGNEW
Ace Boss

ZEENUT SERIES P.C. LEAGUE AGNEW VERNON

SAM AGNEW AND THE SAN DIEGO ACES. A four-team Southern California Class D League formed quickly in 1929. San Diego got a franchise and the team was named the Aces. Their manager was former American League catcher Sam Agnew. The Aces quickly took command of the league. It was clear that team owner CH "Doc" Atkins and Agnew had done a remarkable job filling the San Diego roster with quality players on short notice. Unfortunately, the ill-conceived league drew "aces and eights" and would not last through the summer months. By sweeping a doubleheader against the San Bernardino Padres on judgment day, San Diego finished in first place when the tents were folded in June. Even Coronado got a team. Appropriately, it was named the Ventura-Orange County-Pomona-San Clemente-Coronado Arabs. That has to be a record for team relocation. Strangely, it was the Bakersfield club that quit the league before the Arabs could.

SAN DIEGO ACES UNIFORMS. Although there are not any pictures of the San Diego Aces team, the George Harding San Diego All-Stars are shown wearing their uniforms. The All-Stars won their league championship in the winter of 1929 and performed well against Los Angeles clubs. Note the configuration of "S" and "D" on the jerseys. San Diego High School had previously used this design.

SEVEN

"Dreams Materialize"

1930–1936

San Diego Population: 147,995
Weather: Sunny, 72 degrees

Late in January of 1930, Harry Jacobs organized a collection of San Diego's finest players to challenge the California Winter League teams. Harry should have gone fishing instead. The Philadelphia Royal Giants and Pirrone's All-Stars had fun pounding the local boys. On the local winter scene, Western Dairies, like the cream in their milk, finished on top of the City League. Showley Brothers Candy Company won the "gonfalon" in the Commercial Indoor League with a 26-16 rout of San Diego Electric Railway. (Gonfalon: n. a flag hanging from a crosspiece instead of an upright staff, usually ending in streamers; esp., such a standard of any of the medieval republics of Italy.)

In March, the PCL Playoff Champion Hollywood Stars returned for spring training at Navy Field. Fans generally enjoyed the Coast League exhibition games. They even got to see the Chicago Cubs nip the Sheiks (another nickname for the Hollywoods), 4-3, in 11 innings. San Diego High School won its third consecutive SCIF championship with an 8-0 victory over Cathedral High School of Los Angeles.

Sandlot ball was bigger than ever. Encinitas captured the Inter-County championship with a 7-1 triumph over the Marines. The Devil Dogs were an outstanding team with several players from the 1929 Mare Island national service championship club. Bert Ritchey's Colored Colts lost a 9-3 game to the National City nine that went on to claim the Inter-City League title with a decisive 17-6 triumph over the Army. Morgan's Dairy edged Stubbs Motors, 9-8, for the City loop title. George Harding's All-Stars won several games against top competition like the LA Colored Giants, the Ventura Athletic Club, and the Navy All-Stars. Immediately following the September 6 game at Navy Field, lights were erected for night football.

Linn Platner entered a solid team of primarily local talent in the 1931 California Winter League. The San Diegans opened the season with a 1-0 victory over the Nashville Elite Colored Giants on January 11. They dominated the El Paso Mexicans and Pirrone's All-Stars in league play. Platner's team hosted the Giants for the three-game championship series in February. Nashville won the first two games to claim the title. Their star, Willie Bobo, "probably the greatest first baseman his race ever has produced," went to celebrate in Tijuana. It is believed

113

he drank wood alcohol in a honky tonk. When teammates checked the next morning, he was found dead in his hotel room.

Regardless, the teams decided to play a meaningless and listless game, which San Diego won. The man known as "the Black Sisler" was gone. His good friend Dewey Creacy mourned, "That was the trouble with Willie. He was always seekin' around for liquor. He bought some cheap alcohol and now I keep lookin' over to first base after him, and Bobo ain't there no more. Can't hardly play ball without no Bobo on first base." The Giants donated their share of the gate receipts from the game to ship Bobo's body to his mother in Mineral Wells, Tennessee.

In March, Billy Evans, general manager of the Cleveland Indians, visited San Diego to explore the possibility of moving his club's spring training camp from New Orleans. He watched Oscar Vitt put the Hollywood Stars through their paces at Navy Field. As the scenario unfolded, Louisiana Governor Huey "Kingfish" Long got involved in delicate negotiations and convinced the Indians to remain in the Crescent City. Apparently the persuasive Kingfish designated the entire Indians front office as honorary members of his official staff.

A headline read: "Fat Men Down North Parkers In Wild Game." These were not the same nineteenth century civic porkers who played for fun and charity. Magee's Fat Men, a talented barnstorming troupe out of the Imperial Valley, were "husky in name only." Sponsored by the Fat Men Company, the Magees featured the Willingham Brothers of Brawley. Rod Luscomb's North Park club was well stocked with former SDHS talent like Athos Sada, Tony Galasso, Ashley Joerndt, and Fernando Villarino. The Fat Men were better and prevailed, 14-12.

A new, powerful City League that incorporated the best teams of the former City and Inter-City Leagues was formed in April. The significance of this development was that it would play its schedule throughout the summer months. Good ball was played at this level, but it did not fill San Diego's appetite for professional baseball.

In reality, it was Linn Platner's semi-pro San Diego team that drew the fans and coverage. The novelty of night baseball at Navy Field caused the most excitement that summer. San Diego played half a dozen games under the lights with Joe E. Brown's All-Stars. On July 8, "Filmdom's big-mouthed funny man, Joe E. Brown, demonstrated his comics and baseball ability at the same time as he led his major and minor league all-stars to a 4 to 1 triumph over Linn Platner's San Diegans in the second of a two-game series before more than 2000 fans at Navy Field last night." San Diego had won the first contest, 11-1, and the teams split the rest of the schedule.

Irrepressible former major leaguer Carl Sawyer and his Pirrone All-Stars continued the comedy when the Browns returned to Hollywood. In the throes of the Great Depression, America enjoyed laughter and light entertainment to balance the despair. The Platners played serious ball as well. San Diego whitewashed the LA Nippons, 11-0, lost a close game to the mighty Philadelphia Royal Giants, 2-1, and bounced back to beat the Nogales Internationals of the Arizona-Texas League, 5-3.

When the Royal Giants returned to town for a two-game series in November, San Diego was knotted with Philadelphia for first place in California's Winter League. Satchel Paige and Rube Foster's younger brother, "Cannonball" Willie Foster, were able to hold San Diego in check. "Cool Papa" Bell and "Mule Suttles, the Babe Ruth of colored baseball," provided the offense for the Royals. With a 22-2 record, the Giants ran away with the title. The pitching match-up of the year was the simultaneous one-hit gems thrown by Satchel Paige and San Diego's own, Gook Nielsen. Philadelphia won the game, 1-0. The *Pittsburgh Courier* was duly impressed: "This was the greatest game ever played at White Sox Park [Los Angeles]."

Hollywood was back in San Diego for "spring training 1932." They played a mixed schedule that included exhibitions with the San Diego town team and the San Diego State freshmen team. Speculation continued that the Stars would move to San Diego because of the on-going squabbles between Bill Lane and his Wrigley Field landlords. The rumors had become a familiar refrain. The Angels would squeeze, Lane would threaten to move and Los Angeles would back off.

114

Neighborhood House defeated the Agua Caliente sponsored Braves for the City League championship. On April 20, under the lights before 500 shivering fans, San Diego slipped past the Hollywood Girls, 7-6. It was decided to wait until the weather warmed to play more night games at Navy Field. Later, on a balmy summer night beside the bay, Linn Platner's San Diegans pushed a run across in the eleventh inning to edge the Philadelphia Royal Giants, 4-3. It was part of an extended nine-game series. San Diego had taken the first six games and the Royal Giants were lucky to salvage the last three contests.

Los Angeles Leonard Wood American Legion Post 125 captured the 1932 Southern California championship from Hoover coach Wofford Caldwell's "Fighting Bobs" Legion team. Several members of Post 125 would sign professional contracts, including Bobby Doerr, George McDonald, Steve Mesner, Al Lyons, and Mickey Owen. Doerr, McDonald, Mesner, and Lyons would all become future Lane Field Padres.

In sandlot action, City League champion North Park proved to be the best in San Diego County when they humiliated the Bay League champs, Old Town, 17-0, on the victor's playground. Attendance had been down, but this December game drew the largest crowd of the season. Once again, all-purpose Navy Field was unavailable because it was now being used for football and motorcycle races. Tennis balls, polo ponies, and soccer all had their moments at the foot of Broadway. It was feared baseball had lost its appeal in San Diego.

On February 9, 1933, *San Diego Union* Sports Editor Ted Steinmann wrote, "Baseball is 'out' in the city schools of San Diego starting next year, unless those who want the game to continue, will turn out and help the sport pay for itself." It was a well known fact that football paid for the highly respected baseball program at San Diego High School. There were individuals in the education system who did not like baseball.

Physical Education Superintendent WA Kearns said, "In baseball, you know, razzing the umpire, opposing players, in fact anyone connected with the game, is considered just a part of the sport. In any other sport, such conduct as the crowd stamping its feet or calling out seeking to unnerve a boy pitcher at a critical point in the game, would be considered unsportsmanlike." Was this bean counter a golfer? Baseball at the junior high level had already been discontinued.

Arthur S. Billings, former coach of the Navy's Fleet Air team, took umbrage. He responded to another educator's recommendations in a letter to the *Union*: "I would suggest that if you cannot organize your department in such a manner as to include baseball, you should tender your resignation and let one of the army of unemployed assume control." Despite the controversy, 121 boys turned out for baseball at San Diego High School.

Somehow, in the middle of the Depression, a new ballpark was built in the Midway area near the Causeway. Unfortunately, the Hollywood Stars decided to move their spring training operations to Long Beach. But San Diego did have the Hollywood Theatre baseball team that was anxious to book games with service teams. Did the strippers and fan dancers double as cheerleaders for the Hollywood Theatre?

Newly elected Franklin Delano Roosevelt was invited to attend the Opening Day game between the Washington Senators and Philadelphia Athletics. The president "inquired about the sale of beer in the parks." Heydler said his league would permit bars in the stands where they were allowed prior to prohibition, but no sales would be allowed in the seats." Prohibition ended on April 7, 1933. Let's raise a glass to FDR! While we are at it, let's hoist another mug of suds for that long forgotten minor league pitcher, Harry Horton, the only player in baseball history to be traded for a bottle of beer.

It turned out that baseball was played at San Diego High School. The Hilltoppers won the Pomona Invitational Tournament and Chet Smith won a special trophy provided by Babe Ruth for hitting five home runs in four games. Chet and his brother, Henry "Swede" Smith, pitched for Mike Morrow's championship team. Then San Diego had to forfeit all of its games and a chance for another SCIF title when it was learned that "two members inadvertently played in a sandlot game last June." Chet and Henry Smith were the guilty parties. They admitted to have played sandlot ball under assumed names. How "inadvertent" is an assumed name?

This gave crosstown Hoover the opportunity to shine. For the first time in school history, the Cardinals reached the 1933 SCIF championship game against Santa Maria. Minus the services of injured star pitcher Don Kimball, the Redbirds fell 9-1 to the Saints. Hoover had a good team that included catcher Woody Helm, first baseman Frank Green, shortstop Don Ransom, and outfielder Morris "Moose" Siraton. Green had raced home to score Hoover's only run against Santa Maria. That same day in Ohio, 17-year-old Jesse Owens ran a 9.4 second world record 100-yard dash at a high school track.

A local CCC baseball league was organized for their young workers throughout the county. The participating Civilian Conservation Corps camps included Cuyamaca, Fallbrook, Lyons Valley, Minnewawa, Pamo, Pine Valley, Puerto la Cruz, San Diego River, and Temecula. Minnewawa would whip Temecula for the district championship.

Sandlot ball had grown to be bigger and more popular than ever. Although school administrators continued to argue that baseball was too costly, it was a favorite sport during the Depression because it was so inexpensive. Teams somehow found money to travel throughout the county to participate in far flung leagues.

The City League, which included three Navy ships, stretched all the way to Escondido. Arterburn & Mills Auctioneers won the first half and Escondido, with a big league infield of Babe Dahlgren and the Coscarart Brothers (Joe, Steve and Pete), took the second half. On March 4, 1934, A&M won the championship with a 4-0 victory over the Grape Pickers. The Auctioneers were without the services of star outfielder Athos Sada who had gone to Riverside for a tryout with the Hollywood Stars. Arterburn & Mills added the County title with a 6-0 triumph over County League winners, Ocean Beach.

Hoover showed San Diego High that 1933 was not a fluke. In an early season game, "Williams, an unsung sophomore outfielder, batting from the south side of the plate, tripled and scored on Kimball's single to left." Young Ted Williams went 2 for 5 that day as the Cardinals won, 3-1. The Hilltoppers rebounded to win the Pomona 20–30 Club title, but failed to take their league. Hoover returned to the SCIF title game, but lost, 6-3, to Cathedral of Los Angeles. Williams was used sparingly in tournament play, but against Pasadena, he "propelled the ball over the right field fence, but to the right of the 'barber pole,' the hit going only for a double." (Hoover had a short right field.) The Cardinals found a new shortstop on the basketball team in 1934. He was Johnny "Swede" Jensen who would go on to play ten seasons with the PCL Padres.

CWA kicked and balked its way to a 4-3 triumph over American Legion Post 6 in an "exciting and dull" donkey baseball game at Sports Field (Navy Field). The winning run scored from first on a single. Apparently Frank Larkin had previous donkey jockey experience as he navigated his burro around the bases to home plate. The highlight of the game was watching Legionnaire Ryan's wild home run ride around the infield. Donkey ball never really did catch on in San Diego. It was too pastoral for the locals.

Summer days and nights were now filled with sandlot baseball and a relatively new phenomenon: Softball. San Diego boasted Double A, Single A, Double B, Bankers, and Girls Leagues. Independent teams included among other clubs, the Van Camp Seconds, Radio Doctors, Thearle's Music, and the Tribune Mail Room. Everyone was playing fast pitch softball. In September, the Van Camp Company held its own championship. The Chickens of the Sea faced the Tunas. The results are unknown.

The Padres were making headlines on San Diego sports pages. They were a football team—an American Legion football team—and they were good. Their roster included former college, high school, and service gridders. Games were played at Sports Field.

On October 28, 1934, 3,000 fans turned out to watch a sandlot game on the University Heights diamond. Walter Church's Service Station beat Rod Luscomb's North Park team, 4-3, behind the brilliant three-hit pitching of San Diego State left-hander, Wilson Hunt. The Aztec hurler had entered the game in relief of Powerene starter Grover Cleveland Alexander. Yes, Grover Cleveland Alexander himself. . . . "Old Pete" had been roughed up for three runs and headed for a quick shower in the second inning. But there were no showers at the playground. The cost to put broken-down Alexander in a Walter Church uniform is unknown, but it is known that Pete put those 3,000 people in the stands. Rod Luscomb, who ran the recreation programs at University Heights, was the beneficiary of this large box office payoff.

Obviously, the other playgrounds did not like this arrangement. WA Kearns, now superintendent of San Diego playgrounds, canceled City League games in December. On January 21, 1935, Kearns removed booking privileges from the San Diego County Baseball Managers Association and personally assumed scheduling control for all playgrounds. Kearns meant business. "I'm going to talk turkey with you fellows. This association is playing with fire in attempting to conduct games in which four professional teams, all members of the City league, are permitted to participate under the banner of your organization. The association must clean house and do away with pro ball. If it does not, the playground commission will organize a City league of its own and conduct it on an amateur basis."

The managers responded quickly. It had long been their custom to offer stipends to pitchers and, furthermore, they claimed most of the players actually worked for their sponsors during the week. The matter was referred to the city manager and city council. Part of the problem was that San Diego did not have a "regular ball park" for winter baseball. A compromise was reached and league play resumed.

In the early going of San Diego's top adult league, Colored Mission Stars shortstop P. Simpson was leading the county with a .545 batting average. Future Padres outfielder Manuel Hernandez was hitting .384 for Cramer's Bakery, and 16-year-old Ted Williams was a .300 hitter for San Diego Market. Tragedy struck in February when "popular Negro character" Henry Grant, manager of the Mission Stars, suddenly died. Grant "was known to just about every fan in the county." Friends in the San Diego County Baseball Managers Association rallied to promote a benefit game to help support his ailing widow. The Stars would face the powerful Texas Liquor Store team with a secret weapon; Satchel Paige would pitch for the Mission Stars.

One thousand fans showed up at Balboa Stadium on Washington's Birthday to watch the masterful Paige turn the Liquor Store bats into useless accessories. "Singin' Satchel Paige" allowed but three hits and struck out 15 Texans en route to a 4-0 shutout. In addition to spinning a brilliant game, Satch sang several songs and was described as "a fine crooner." The SERA band also performed and prizes were given to the patrons.

There was talk to organize another Class D league in Southern California. St. Louis Cardinals vice president Branch Rickey was reportedly interested in placing a team in San Diego. Bitterness remained from the ill-fated Southern California League, which left numerous outstanding debts including unpaid player salaries from 1929. Baseball Commissioner Kenesaw Mountain Landis quickly shot the new league down.

The City of San Diego transferred 25 acres of bay shore property at the foot of Fifth Avenue to the US Navy for a new athletic complex. It became known as Navy Field. The facility would be used over the years for baseball, football, tennis, handball, and physical education. The Navy generously shared these playing fields with San Diego.

High School baseball was again very competitive in 1935. Because his home was on the school district borderline, Ted Williams could have played baseball for Mike Morrow at San Diego High School. He chose Hoover because he wanted to be a pitcher. Ted would lead the Cardinals in hitting that year with a .588 batting average. He went 4-2 on the mound. Among his Hoover teammates were lifelong friends, Del Ballinger (.423) and Roy Engle (.304). Ballinger, a gifted prankster, would later play for the Padres. Engle is better known as a star football player for the University of Southern California. He returned to his high school alma mater to become the Cardinals gridiron coach.

Good as Hoover was, they were unable to knock off San Diego. The Hilltoppers won the consolation prize at the Pomona 20–30 Tournament and rallied to eliminated the Cardinals in the SCIF playoffs with a 14-11 victory. In that game, Ted Williams's three-run homer put Hoover ahead in the sixth inning, but Ted surrendered seven runs in the eighth. The Cavemen placed a tenth Southern California baseball trophy in their crowded showcase.

On June 7, Williams, pitching for Walter Church, threw a three-hitter against the Metropolitan All-Stars. Teddy smacked a triple and a couple of doubles as the Service Station attendants prevailed, 3-1. The starting pitcher for the All-Stars (Kettle) struck out the first seven batters he faced. Kettle was replaced by future big league pitcher Joe Orrell of National City.

Three San Diego area high school boys were honored with selection to the Southern California all-star team. The players were Bill Skelley of San Diego, Woody Helm of Hoover, and Escondido's Karl Hoffman. They received small gold baseballs.

The San Diego Marines took a pair of games from UCLA and dumped Stanford, 6-1. Texas Liquor blasted the Tokyo Giants, 13-3. The touring Japanese came back in the second game of their Sunday doubleheader to whip the San Diego Whippets, 4-1. The beating by Texas Liquor was the worst the Giants suffered on their trip to America. The third day, 17-year-old Russian Victor Starffin won a pitcher's duel with "Sailor Tex" Reichert and the Tokyo Giants shut out the USS *Dobbins*, 2-0.

Service baseball enjoyed a large and captive following in San Diego. The Dobbins bombarded the USS *Salt Lake City*, 27-2, to claim the Scouting Force championship. Reichert, who went 4 for 6 at the plate, pitched the Dobbins to victory on the Marine Base diamond. In sandlot ball, Ocean Beach had its string of 23 straight victories snapped by Texas Liquor.

Bill Skelley, a future Lane Field Padres infielder, tossed a perfect game for San Diego American Legion Post 6 against San Bernardino. San Diego would again meet Leonard Wood of Los Angeles for the Southern California title. LA won the championship, 6-5. Future major leaguers on the Leonard Wood team were Jerry Priddy, Eddie Malone, and Cliff Dapper.

Fisher's Negro Ghosts of Sioux City, Iowa, were the first known traveling softball team to visit San Diego. "The Ghosts are reported to play a fast brand of softball and to specialize in comic antics and a 'ghost ball' demonstration which they give before regular games." They would meet a Double A team, Kerrigan's Jewelers, at Central Playground. Results of the game were not given—too bad. Modern fans would be curious to read about the exploits of a shortstop named Mickey Mouse and an outfield of Bull Fields, Speedy, and PeeWee Williams.

Cramer's Bakery won the City League. Ted Williams played with Walter Church, which evolved into Rod Luscomb's Cardinals. These things were always mercurial. His teammates were SDHS, Hoover, and St. Augustine players. They included Bill Skelley, Frank Galindo, Woody Helm, and Charlie Strada. The San Diego girls softball team made it to the Southern California Championships. At new Navy Field, the USS *Ranger* sank the USS *Memphis*, 7-5.

Hollywood Stars owner Bill Star was whining again. His new plan was to return to Salt Lake City after a 10-year hiatus because, "Salt Lake City hasn't been so hard hit as the California towns." Health concerns were also cited for this possible move. Pacific Coast League officials were scheduled to meet on December 15, 1935, to address this and other issues. San Diego's best chance for professional ball that year would happen the same day when Reuben Verdugo's Escondido Grape Pickers met Joe Pirrone's All-Stars in the opening game of the California Winter League season.

The first item of business at the Coast League meetings in Oakland was to elect a new president. Two days later, William C. Tuttle, a former newspaper man and western novel writer, was the surprise selection. WC Tuttle had been a semi-professional ballplayer in his youth and later, a part-time scout who developed connections with organized baseball. He would prove to be a strong advocate for a Coast League team in San Diego.

On December 20, the *San Diego Union* reported that the San Francisco Mission Reds would relocate to San Diego if a suitable ballpark could be built. There was an air of urgency, because Fresno was actively pursuing the Mission team. This all had a familiar ring, but in lock step, the local newspapers began a relentless campaign to pledge public support for a PCL team. Things got serious when city and port officials conferred and devised a plan for the Works Progress Administration to finance their project. A new ballpark was envisioned on the site of Sports

Field. The WPA would cover 80 percent of the costs, roughly $16,000, and local government would be responsible for the remaining $4,000. The Missions group preferred a wooden ballpark, because concrete would be too cold for night games on the bay.

On Christmas Day 1935, the Philadelphia Royal Giants (AKA: Elite Giants) pummeled Verdugo's charges, 13-9. Henry Smith and Joe Dobbins each had collected two hits off the usually unhittable Satchel Paige. Fifteen hundred fans watched the game at Balboa Stadium. In addition to Paige, this edition of the Giants was loaded with Negro League stars like Turkey Stearnes, Mule Settles, Schoolboy Griffith, Biz Mackey, One Wing White, Sammy Hughes, Felton Snow, Wild Bill, and Zollie Wright. This would be the last of the great "colored teams" to play in the California Winter League.

In his final column of the year, *San Diego Union* Sports Editor Ted Steinmann urged San Diegans to help the Chamber of Commerce bring the San Francisco Missions to town. He warned that time was growing short to land the PCL team.

On January 28, 1936, Steinmann and the *Union* announced an unexpected grand slam. Bill Lane was prepared to move his Hollywood Stars to San Diego. The following day, the headline was straightforward: "City's Dreams Materialize As Ball Pact Signed."

Base ball in San Diego would never be the same . . .

BILL LANE, OSCAR VITT, AND LINN PLATNER. The PCL Playoff Champion Hollywood Stars returned to Navy Field for spring training in 1930. Team owner William "Hardrock Bill" Lane (left) is shown with Stars manager Oscar Vitt and Navy Field manager Linn Platner in this photo taken at the ballpark on March 3, 1930. (Courtesy San Diego Historical Society, SDHS #UT17835.1)

ATHOS SADA AND TONY GALASSO. Athos "Pino" Sada and Tony Galasso were two of the many stars on coach Mike Morrow's 1930 powerhouse Caveman team. In a game against Fullerton, Sada, twin brothers Roy and Ray Holt, and Alan Storton hit consecutive home runs. San Diego High School would go on to win its third consecutive SCIF championship with an 8-0 victory over Cathedral High School of Los Angeles. (Courtesy San Diego Historical Society, SDHS #UT7857 detail)

RYAN CONFECTIONERY. Earl Ryan's Candymen were one of the stronger entries in the San Diego City League. Team members included Chet Harritt, Bill Engeln, Thatcher, Morrison, Kehn, Benninghoven, Evitts, Chounard, Serdynski, Warburton, Marshall, Boykin, Noely, Barclay, and Lawrence Holt. (Courtesy San Diego Historical Society, SDHS Sensor 12-1)

HARBOR DEPARTMENT OFFICES AND SPORTS FIELD. These Lee Passmore photographs show the Harbor Offices building (above) at the corner of Broadway and Harbor Drive and Sports Field (below) as seen looking west across the railroad tracks toward the bay. The Broadway and "B" Street Piers are part of the busy harbor scene. Sports Field had been converted to a football field in this photo. (Courtesy San Diego Historical Society, SDHS #5359-1 detail)

JOE E. BROWN AND THE CAST OF "ALIBI IKE." The novelty of night baseball caused excitement during the summer of 1931. San Diego played half a dozen games under the lights with Joe E. Brown's All-Stars at Navy Field. In the photo, Brown (middle) is flanked by Hollywood Stars Frank Shellenback (far left) and Cedric Durst (far right) on the set of "Alibi Ike." The big-mouthed funny man, a decent player and a great fan, was a frequent visitor to Lane Field and Westgate Park after the Stars moved to San Diego.

1933 HOLLYWOOD STARS. Bill Lane flirted for years with San Diego. His Hollywood Stars held several spring training camps at Navy Field in the late 1920s and early 1930s. Several of the players in this relaxed team photo would become Padres, including Shellenback, Durst, Herm "Old Folks" Pillette (back row, far left), Wally "Preacher" Hebert (second left), and Les Cook (middle row, fourth from left).

TED WILLIAMS AND HOOVER HIGH SCHOOL BASEBALL. Ted Williams lived on the borderline between Hoover and San Diego high schools. He chose to attend Hoover so he could pitch. After a promising sophomore year in 1934 with the Cardinals, Teddy would go on to bat .588 in 1935. His teammates included future Lane Field Padres Johnny "Swede" Jensen and Del Ballinger. Williams is the tall bean pole in the middle of the back row. Though loud and boisterous, Ted was well-liked growing up on San Diego baseball diamonds.

BILL SKELLEY AND SAN DIEGO HIGH SCHOOL BASEBALL. On the other hand, Bill Skelley was reserved, modest, and considered the top high school prospect in San Diego. Although school administrators wanted to discontinue baseball during the Great Depression, the sport thrived and San Diego High continued to dominate the southland. In 1935, the Cavemen placed their tenth Southern California baseball trophy in the school's showcase. That summer, Skelley, a future Padres infielder, crafted a perfect game for American Legion Post 6 against San Bernardino. He is shown kneeling, almost hiding, in the middle of this picture behind the front row.

123

SATCHEL PAIGE. Over the years, Satchel Paige came to San Diego several times. One of his most memorable visits was in February of 1935, when he pitched for the San Diego Mission Stars against Texas Liquor House. Henry Grant, a "popular Negro character" and manager of the Stars, died suddenly. His friends in the San Diego County Baseball Managers Association rallied to promote a benefit game to help support his ailing widow. One thousand fans showed up at City Stadium on Washington's Birthday to watch the masterful Paige turn the Liquor Store bats into useless accessories. "Singin' Satchel Paige" allowed but three hits and struck out 15 Texans en route to a 4-0 shutout. In addition to spinning a brilliant game, Satch sang several songs and was described as "a fine crooner." The SERA band also performed and prizes were given to the patrons.

WALTER MCCOY. In a 1930s junior high school game, young Walter McCoy (far left), pitched and batted Memorial to a 4-3 triumph over Horace Mann. McCoy's grand slam provided the margin of victory. Walt would go on to become a dominate pitcher for the Chicago American Giants in the Negro Leagues. His father, a non-baseball fan, once allowed him to watch a ball game at Sports Field for 20 minutes. McCoy recalled, "I just remember thinking to myself that I'd like to stay right there for about 20 years."

SPORTS FIELD. Downtown San Diego did not have much of a skyline when this game was played at Sports Field during the middle 1930s. The most prominent landmarks are (left to right) San Diego Trust, Bank of America, San Diego Hotel, Santa Fe Depot, and San Diego Gas & Electric. The third baseman is Pete Grijalva.

TEXAS LIQUOR HOUSE. Ocean Beach had run off a string of 23 consecutive victories when they faced Texas Liquor on May 26, 1935. Dick Tallemante shut out the Beachers, 5-0. This photo was autographed to Chet Smith by Joe Grosher (sponsor) and Abe Goldberg (manager). They wrote, "the best shortstop in San Diego, Calif."

BARONA BASE BALL TEAM. Indians began playing base ball in San Diego County during the 1890s. Well into the 1950s, the Barona team would challenge city teams to visit the reservation. Top level amateur baseball continues to be played at Barona. (Courtesy San Diego Historical Society, SDHS #95:19388-1)

PALA MISSIONS. The Pala Warriors were a tough North County team in the early part of the twentieth century. In 1935, the Pala Missions and Barona were members of the San Diego County League along with Ramona, Mesa Grande, Oceanside, and the Escondido Aztecas. (Courtesy King Freeman.)

CRAMER'S BAKERY. Cramer's Bakery sponsored baseball teams for years in San Diego. The 1935 City League championship team included Hudson, Calac, Bailey, Curtis, Lamm, Vidal, Gloss, Cyr, Hill, and Manuel Hernandez.

EL CAJON TEAM. The leading team in the 1935 San Diego winter leagues was El Cajon. Pictured, from left to right, are (front row) Traynor, Harris, Myers, Hill, Hunt, and Garcia; (back row) manager Bob Hunter, Lamb, Embelton, Pete Grijalva, Pete Coscarart, Daley, and Bocardo.

REUBEN VERDUGO'S SAN DIEGO TEAM. It appeared the only professional ball San Diego would get to watch in 1936 was Reuben Verdugo's Escondido Grape Pickers in the California Winter League. Shown, from left to right, are Chet Harritt, Bill Bailey, Earle Brucker, Joe Coscarart, and Joe Dobbins. When Bill Lane decided in January to move his Hollywood Stars to San Diego, the fans simply stopped going to the stadium to see Verdugo's team.

NAVY FIELD DEDICATION. In February of 1935, the Navy accepted a 25 acre parcel of land, at the foot of Fifth Avenue, from the City of San Diego for the development of four new diamonds and assorted other sports facilities. The complex was eventually dedicated a month before the opening of Lane Field on the site of old Navy Field. Among the dignitaries present were Admiral Reeves and GA Davidson. (Courtesy San Diego Historical Society, SDHS Sensor 13-102)